# Play Structures & Backyard Fun

### How to Build:
### Playsets • Sports Courts • Games • Swingsets • More

COOL
SPRINGS
PRESS

Inspiring | Educating | Creating | Entertaining

Brimming with creative inspiration, how-to projects, and useful information to enrich your everyday life, Quarto Knows is a favorite destination for those pursuing their interests and passions. Visit our site and dig deeper with our books into your area of interest: Quarto Creates, Quarto Cooks, Quarto Homes, Quarto Lives, Quarto Drives, Quarto Explores, Quarto Gifts, or Quarto Kids.

First published in 2010 by Creative Publishing international, Inc., an imprint of The Quarto Group, 401 Second Avenue North, Suite 310, Minneapolis, MN 55401 USA. This edition published by Cool Springs Press in 2018. T (612) 344-8100 F (612) 344-8692 www.QuartoKnows.com

Cool Springs Press titles are also available at discount for retail, wholesale, promotional, and bulk purchase. For details, contact the Special Sales Manager by email at specialsales@quarto.com or by mail at The Quarto Group, Attn: Special Sales Manager, 401 Second Avenue North, Suite 310, Minneapolis, MN 55401 USA.

10 9 8 7 6 5 4 3 2 1

ISBN: 978-0-7603-6386-7

Library of Congress Control Number: 2018939840

Acquiring Editor: Mark Johanson
Project Manager: Alyssa Bluhm
Art Director: James Kegley
Cover Photo: Shutterstock/Mark Herreid
Layout: Danielle Smith-Boldt

Printed in China

MIX
Paper from responsible sources
FSC® C104723

## NOTICE TO READERS

For safety, use caution, care, and good judgment when following the procedures described in this book. The publisher and BLACK+DECKER cannot assume responsibility for any damage to property or injury to persons as a result of misuse of the information provided.

The techniques shown in this book are general techniques for various applications. In some instances, additional techniques not shown in this book may be required. Always follow manufacturers' instructions included with products, since deviating from the directions may void warranties. The projects in this book vary widely as to skill levels required: some may not be appropriate for all do-it-yourselfers, and some may require professional help.

Consult your local building department for information on building permits, codes, and other laws as they apply to your project.

# Contents

## Play Structures & Backyard Fun

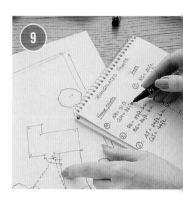

# Contents (Cont.)

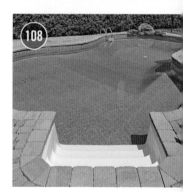

# Introduction

*F*un. That's the whole idea behind backyard recreation structures. Ideally, they aren't just fun to use; projects like the ones in this book are also a blast to plan, design, adapt, and build. At least, that was the criteria used in selecting all the projects included here. If it's not fun, what's the point?

Divided into four common-sense sections, these projects represent an incredible diversity from which you can choose. Big or small, complex or simple, you'll find a project in this book to match any level of DIY expertise and ambition. There is also something for children of every age, from four to forty. Want to give your six-year-old the gift of an incredible hideaway that transforms from a mountaintop pirate's fort to a medieval castle with a flick of the imagination? A clubhouse like the one on page 121 should do the trick. Dad wants to work on his short game on a lazy Saturday afternoon? Look no further than the putting green on page 96. If you have the space, topography, time, and inclination, you can even build several of these projects to define different areas of your backyard for different purposes and groups. A bocce court (page 88) is the perfect anchor for an adult cookout area, where friends can lounge over a cocktail or two. An obstacle course (page 72) on the other side of the yard will keep the kids occupied for many happy hours, while keeping them physically fit.

Unless you're willing to change the look and style of your backyard, you'll find that different landscapes are usually better suited to one project or another. A long, flat driveway is the ideal home for a basketball hoop (page 86) and three-point dream shots, while an expansive, wooded property will be much more accommodating of a zipline (page 60).

If you opt for a project that is targeted to the younger members of the household, include them in the planning and construction. Planning, designing, measuring, marking, cutting, and building can all be great opportunities for young DIYers to hone math skills, learn about basic physics and geometry, and test out their own hypotheses about the way things work. No matter what the project is or who builds it, however, safety should always be the first and foremost concern when it comes to backyard recreation. Wear the proper safety gear whenever you work with power tools or dangerous hand tools. Follow best safety practices in constructing projects and ensure all safety guards are correctly installed in anything you build—this includes those directed in the project steps and common-sense features such as rounding off sharp edges. You'll find more safety information throughout the book, and links to safety organizations in the Resources section on page 141.

# Planning & Basics

Before starting a large project, it's important to get a clear idea of where to build it, what landscaping work is involved, and how much it will cost. If the structure will be anywhere close to the property lines and will be difficult to move after you build it, make sure you know exactly what setbacks are required in your area. Talk to an inspector about what you're planning to do—it doesn't cost anything; in fact, you probably will get some good advice or handouts about construction details, and it might save you from big problems later on.

If you live in an area with a neighborhood homeowner's association, or your house is part of a condominium development, check your deed and talk to your neighbors before starting any permanent or semi-permanent projects to find out if there are restrictions. You'll also need to know how deep to dig footings and what to do if you have bad soil or a high water table. This all sounds worse than it is—one or two phone calls usually resolve all of these questions, and it's best to get the answers at the start.

You also should estimate the cost of materials to avoid surprises. For complicated projects like a treehouse or a large playset, lumberyards and home centers will estimate costs for you if you give them a detailed scale drawing of what you plan to build. It's always a good idea to add 10 percent for waste and mistakes.

## In this chapter:
- Working & Building Safely
- Finding the Right Spot
- Outdoor Building Materials
- Tools

# Working & Building Safely

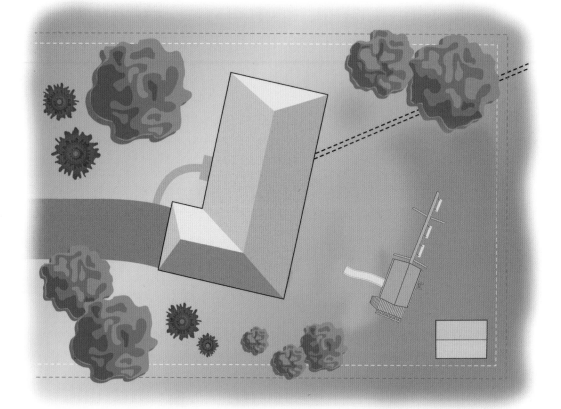

**Before building anything,** locate your lot lines and any buried utilities. Make note of overhead utility lines, and make sure your play structure is far enough away from them so the two don't touch—the general recommendation is to make sure utility lines are at least twice the height of the structure (which includes most building projects, including swingsets). Play areas must be at least 6' from any building, tree, or other obstacle. The clear area in front and back of swings must be at least twice the height of the swingset (measured from the center of the swingset).

**Before buying any lumber,** make scaled construction drawings. It will make buying materials and building the structure much easier and help you avoid expensive mistakes. If you need to obtain a building permit, inspectors will also want to see your construction drawings.

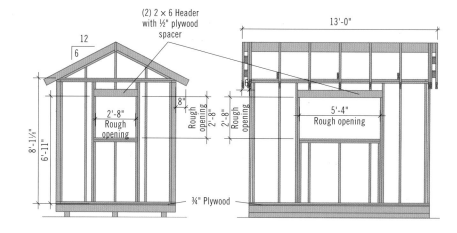

# Safety Equipment

**Protective gloves** play two important roles when you are working outdoors: they protect your hands from abrasions when working with tools or handling building and landscaping materials, and they prevent contact with chemicals such as solvent-based finishing products. Wear well-fitted work gloves whenever they do not interfere with important dexterity concerns. Wear rubber gloves when working with solvent-base paints, stains, and sealers or other chemicals that are not suitable for skin contact.

**Protective eyewear** is perhaps the most important safety gear you can wear. Quality protective eyewear has lightweight, shatterproof lenses that are resistant to fogging. Some are tinted to protect against UV rays. If you will be working around chemicals or airborne irritants, wear safety goggles that fit your face snugly. Some prescription glasses are rated as safety glasses, but don't assume that yours are: wear goggles over them if you are not certain.

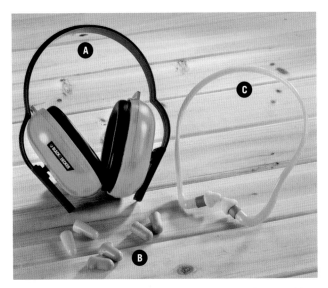

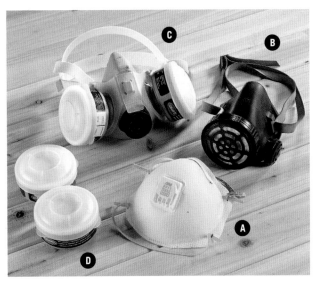

**Wear ear protection** when working with power tools or working around other loud noises. Basic construction earmuffs (A) are inexpensive and reliable. For a slightly higher cost you can purchase electronic versions that feature noise canceling so only objectionable and dangerous noises are blocked. Disposable foam ear plugs (B) will do in a pinch, but they tend to loosen. Foam earplugs connected with a head band (C) stay put longer.

**Respiratory protection** is worn in areas where ventilation is poor or whenever you are cutting treated lumber or working around airborne particulates, noxious gases, or fumes. A paper mask with an N-95 rating and two straps (A) will block particulates such as sawdust, insulation dust, and most allergens. A half mask (B) has replaceable filters that block out additional particles, along with some fumes. A respirator (C) provides the most complete breathing protection. It has interchangeable cartridges (D).

# Finding the Right Spot

After you decide on a project for your yard—but before you buy any supplies—you'll need to figure out exactly how big the project needs to be and then lay it out on the yard to make sure it's going to fit. If you're constructing a large play structure or sports court, draw an accurate site plan of your yard on a sheet of graph paper. If you need a permit, the building department will also require copies. Draw in the property lines, existing structures, trees, gardens, and any other nearby features that may impact your new project. Make sure to note the location and height of overhead utility lines. They should be distant at least twice the height of the swingset or fort; if not, contact an electrician or the utility company about having the utility lines moved or raised.

Make several copies of the site plan, then sketch in the structure you plan to build so you can determine if you have enough clearance, both for the structure and for the activity that will be going on around it. Playgrounds need an additional 6 feet of clearance all the way around the built structure and swingsets have to have clear space from their center equal to twice their height (thus, if the swingset is 8 feet high, you'll need 16 feet of open space on both sides of the beam).

## THE YARD SURVEY

Accurate yard measurements are critical for planning the size and placement of backyard structures. They also help you work out how to level uneven areas, drain wet spots, and landscape. To sketch your survey, follow these steps:

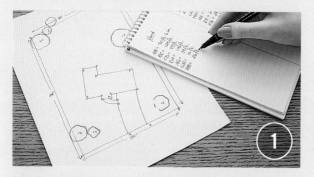

**Sketch your yard** and all its main features on a sheet of paper. Assign a key letter to each point. Measure all straight lines and record the measurements on a notepad.

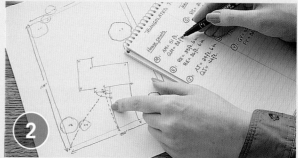

**Take triangulated measurements** to locate other features, such as trees that don't lie along straight lines. Triangulation involves locating a feature by measuring its distance from any two points whose positions are known.

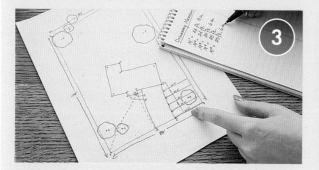

**Plot irregular boundaries and curves,** and note high spots or low-lying areas that need attention. Plot these features by taking a series of perpendicular measurements from a straight reference line, such as the edge of your house or garage.

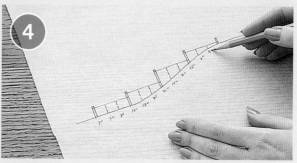

**Sketch elevations to show slopes.** Measure the vertical drop of a slope using different-sized stakes and string. Connect the string to the stakes so it is perfectly horizontal. Measure the distance between the string and ground at 2' intervals along the string.

# Improving Uneven Ground

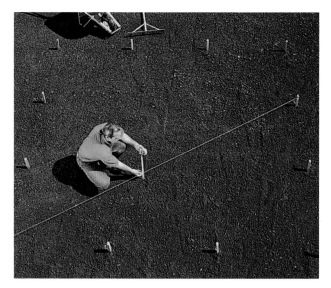

**Create level areas** for playing lawn sports such as croquet, badminton, and bocce. Drive stakes to outline the perimeter of the area you want to level. Run mason's strings between the stakes and level them. Find the high point and add soil to raise the surrounding ground. Or, find the low point and excavate around it.

**Use a hand tamp** to compact the soil you add. Don't overtamp the soil where you'll be planting grass or it could become too dense for a healthy lawn.

 ## How to Improve Drainage

① **Runoff channel**

**Remove a section of sod** and dig a shallow drainage trench sloping to the center, creating a V shape. Use the shovel to smooth the sides as you work.

②

**Replace the sod in the trench,** compressing it against the soil and then thoroughly watering it to create a natural-looking swale.

# Terrace Hillsides with Retaining Walls

**Timbers** are a fast, relatively inexpensive way to build a retaining wall. Fill the space behind them with gravel to keep them dry, and lock the wall against the hillside with T-shaped "deadman" anchors.

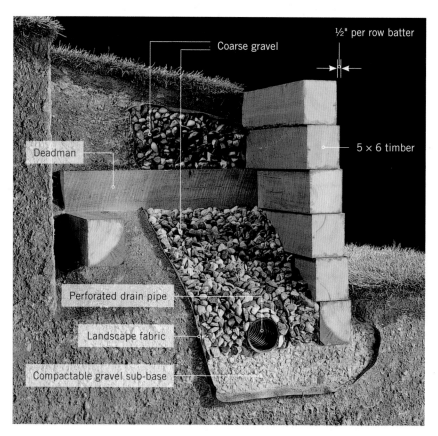

½" per row batter

Coarse gravel

5 × 6 timber

Deadman

Perforated drain pipe

Landscape fabric

Compactable gravel sub-base

**Interlocking blocks** are a permanent solution to a sloping yard. They don't require mortar and are simple to install.

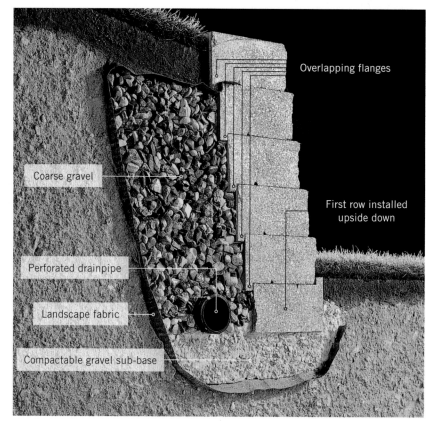

Overlapping flanges

First row installed upside down

Coarse gravel

Perforated drainpipe

Landscape fabric

Compactable gravel sub-base

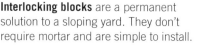

## WHY TERRACE?

Using retaining walls to create terraces in your yard is an effective way to make sloping ground usable for recreational activities.

# SAFE SURFACES

One of the keys to a safe playground is having a surface that cushions your children when they fall. Falls account for approximately three-quarters of all playground injuries, according to the US Consumer Products Safety Commission. Including a safe surface, therefore, is an important part of your play area.

Stay away from hard surfaces such as asphalt, concrete, dirt, and grass. Some of the more common loose-fill materials you can use for your playground include:

**Wood mulch:** Wood mulch is essentially wood that has been chopped into small pieces by a wood chipper. It is available by the truckload or can be purchased by the bag.

**Wood chips:** Wood chips are small pieces of wood, twigs and leaves of similar sizes that have been through a wood chipper. The chips come from tree limbs, branches, and brush. It is also readily available.

**Engineered wood fibers:** This material is uniformly sized shredded hardwood fibers.

**Sand:** Both fine sand and coarse sand can be used for playground surfaces. Sand is fairly inexpensive; however, it's easily displaced and gets in children's clothing.

**Pea gravel:** Pea gravel is small round pieces of washed gravel, generally less than $\frac{3}{8}$" in diameter. Gravel is less likely to attract animals than sand or wood. The disadvantage is that gravel can freeze together and become hard in freezing temperatures.

**Shredded tires:** Shredded tires are just that: shredded tires. They have superior shock-absorbing qualities and will not deteriorate over time. Be sure to use shredded tires that do not contain wire from steel-belted tires and that have been treated to keep them from discoloring clothing.

Each of these surfaces is relatively easy to install in a play area. Apply the material you choose to a depth of 12" and extend it at least 70" in all directions from the play equipment for maximum protection against falls. For swings, the surface should extend to a distance twice the height of the swings both in front and in back of each swing. If you have an 8' swing, for instance, cushion a surface that extends 16' in front and in back of the swing.

You'll either need to build a retaining barrier or dig a pit to contain the surface material. The area should have good drainage so the material doesn't sit in water. Most surfaces need periodic maintenance, such as grading or adding more material to keep an adequate depth.

Wood mulch

Wood chips

Engineered wood fibers

Sand

Pea gravel

Shredded tires

# Outdoor Building Materials

Backyard recreational structures have to stand up to years of hard use and hard weather, and any material used to make them must be both sturdy and rot- or rust-resistant.

Generally, the least expensive and most widely available wood used for exterior structures is pressure-treated pine (here, "pine" typically includes several evergreen species related to pine, including spruce and fir). Current treatment solutions for preserving wood include C-A (Copper Azole), ACQ (Alkaline Copper Quartenary), and Borate. All may be used for any backyard application as long as the wood will not be exposed to salt water on a regular basis. If your wood is green-treated (C-A or ACQ), you must use hot-dipped, galvanized fasteners that are made of triple-dipped, stainless steel, or specially coated screws approved for treated wood. Green-treated wood products cause metal to corrode rapidly, which can lead to premature structural failure if you use unapproved metal hardware. CCA, the controversial arsenic-based treatment chemical, was pulled from the market several years ago.

Cedar, which is naturally rot-resistant, is sold at most lumberyards and home centers, though in some

areas it may be available only through special order. Although cedar generally costs more than treated pine, it will not last as long as treated lumber if it's in contact with the ground (you can increase cedar's rot resistance by treating it with wood preservative). Often, builders will use treated pine to construct structural members such as posts and framing, and then use cedar, which is warmer and more attractive, for decking, railings, and trim.

Other naturally rot-resistant woods sometimes sold at lumberyards are redwood, cypress, and ipé (a South American wood), but these are not as widely available and can be prohibitively expensive.

Composite and plastic lumber suitable for exterior projects are sold in increasing quantities and selections at home centers and lumberyards. It's more expensive than treated wood but has a perfectly smooth appearance and won't warp, crack, or splinter as it ages. It's an excellent choice for trim and decking, but it is not rated for structural use. Decking must be supported every 16 inches to avoid sagging. This type of lumber can be cut and drilled just like wood but may require different fasteners, so check the instructions when you buy it.

**Cedar and pressure-treated pine** are used frequently for building recreational structures, but composite boards and other species of wood can be used effectively under some conditions. Wood and wood-based products for outdoor building include: Douglas fir (A), cedar (B), pressure-treated pine (C), hollow composite material (D), solid composite material (E).

**Use exterior-rated fasteners for outdoor projects.** Shown here is a sampling of outdoor fasteners and hardware: Triple-dipped galvanized joist hangers (A); galvanized/exterior-rated carriage bolts, lag bolts, washers and nuts (B); triple-dipped galvanized post standoffs (C); galvanized corner brackets (D); joist-hanger nails (E); coated deck screws in various lengths (F); galvanized common nails (G).

## HAULING MATERIALS

You can save delivery charges (usually $35 to $50) and control delivery times by hauling landscape materials yourself in a pickup or trailer. The yard workers at the supply center will load your vehicle free of charge with a front-end loader or skid loader. Do not overload your vehicle. Although most operators are aware of load limits, they will typically put in as much as you tell them to. As a general rule of thumb, a compact truck (roughly the size of a Ford Ranger) can handle one scoop of dirt, sand or gravel, which is about ¾ of a cubic yard; a half-ton truck (Ford F-150) will take a scoop and a half (a little over a cubic yard), and a three-quarter ton truck (F-250) can haul two scoops (one and a half cubic yards) safely. Be sure to check the gross vehicle weight and payload data label on the driver's door.

# Tools

Most of the projects in this book can be built with standard construction and yard tools, but you may want to rent specialty tools on a project-by-project basis. Everything from small hand tools and power tools to front-end loaders are available at tool rental stores, and it's well worth a visit or a look at a rental catalog to see what's available. Although rentals can be expensive, they can literally save days of hard labor, not to mention sore backs.

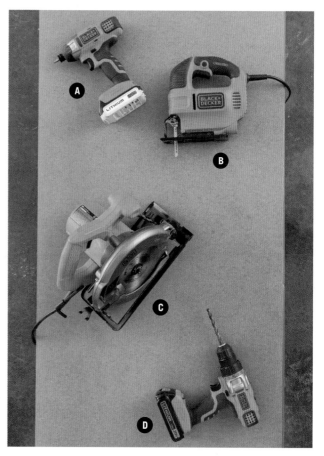

A few of the hand power tools you'll need for just about any backyard building project include an impact driver (A), a jigsaw (B), a circular saw (C), and a drill/driver (D).

Pneumatic tools include: air compressor (A), framing-nail gun (B), air hammer with chisel bits (C), finish-nail gun (D), air hose (E).

**A two-person power auger** makes quick work of posthole digging. Be sure to have your property inspected and flagged for underground lines before you dig.

Specialty tools include: tamping machines (A), sod cutter (B), power auger (C), hand tamper (D), chainsaw (E).

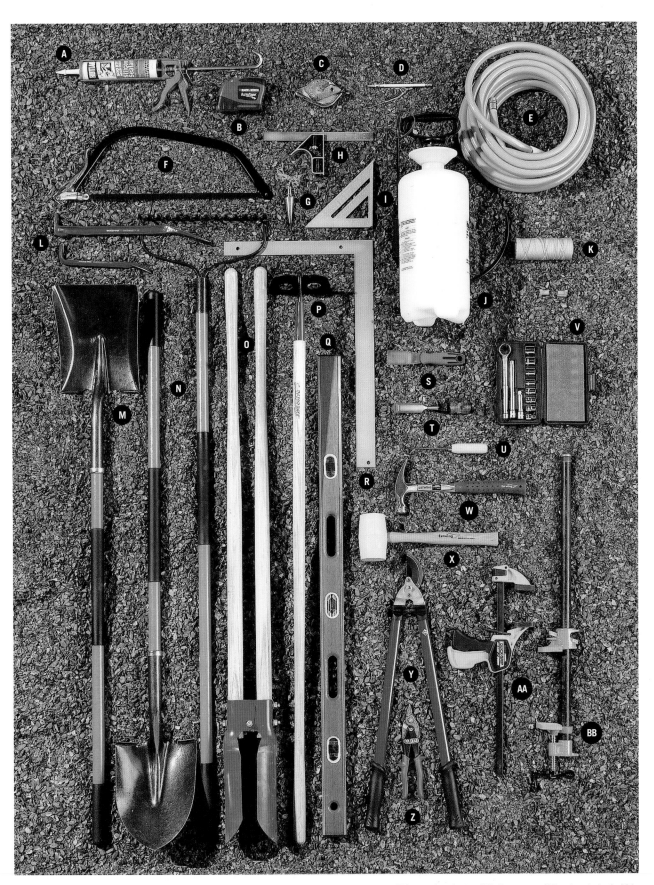

**Hand tools include:** caulk gun (A), tape measure (B), chalk line (C), compass (D), garden hose (E), bow saw (F), plumb bob (G), combination square (H), speed square (I), pressure sprayer (J), mason's line (K), pry bars (L), square and round shovels (M), garden rake (N), posthole digger (O), hoe (P), carpenter's level (Q), framing square (R), putty knife (S), wood chisel (T), awl (U), socket wrench (V), hammer (W), rubber mallet (X), pruning shears (Y), metal shears (Z), bar clamps (AA), pipe clamps (BB).

# Play Structures

A t a time when technology dominates children's lives, a place for them to enjoy pure, unadulterated play is more essential than ever. Simple, physical play is not only great exercise, but it's also a key part of childhood, one of the joys of literally not having a care in the world.

Sure, you can head to the nearest park or school playground, but just how often can you honestly say you'll do that? The much better option is a backyard play structure, one that kids can enjoy on a whim and that you can supervise with a cool drink in your hand and a hamburger on the grill.

The right play structure isn't necessarily the biggest or fanciest. It's the one that is best suited to the age, abilities, and preferences of your child. That usually means choosing a playset design based on the age of the children that will use it most. Low platforms and easily gripped features will be much better for younger children, while older kids can safely face the challenges of a more vertical structure, one that includes a high slide, ladder-access fort, or monkey bars.

No matter the size or complexity of the unit you build, it has to be safe. That starts with the base you set down underneath the play structure and continues through every detail of construction. You'll find all the fine points of play-structure safety in the pages that follow, and you'll also find a look at the different options for building one. You can buy precut systems that take all the guesswork out of the project in exchange for a significantly higher price tag, or you can build your own design from scratch. That will entail a lot more work but will also yield the satisfaction that the play structure is tailored to your children and their friends.

## In this chapter:
- Choosing a Play System
- Playground Safety
- Precut Playground Kit
- DIY Playset
- DIY Swingset

# Choosing a Play System

You have several options when it comes to making your backyard a kid's paradise. You can always go the quick and easy route by having professionals do the whole project for you, soup to nuts. Of course, that can set you back quite a bit of money. Fortunately, if you're the roll-up-your-sleeves type, there are plenty of other options to getting a play structure built. Pick the right option for you, your budget, and your skills.

**Hire a playground builder.** This is the simplest option. A number of local and national companies offer a wide range of models, from basic play areas to small mansions, that they will build and install. The advantage of hiring one of these companies is that they have experience, use high-quality materials, offer dozens of fun options, are up-to-date on all the codes and safety features, guarantee their work, and they don't require anything from you except money. The

disadvantage is that it can be a lot of money—three to four times as much as a comparable precut package that you assemble yourself.

**Buy a precut package.** This option is the simplest and most failsafe for the DIYer. The playground is already designed, all the pieces are cut (although some packages require you to buy additional standard lengths of lumber), and all accessories and hardware are included. You'll have to dig holes and do some drilling and bolting, but other than that you just follow the instructions. Most companies offer a number of options and add-ons, so you can usually get everything you and your children want in a playground. Plus, the safety features are all designed in. The disadvantage is that you're paying several times the cost of the materials for someone to design the playground and cut and package all the pieces for you.

**A playset structure** is the heart of any backyard playground. Choosing the model you want is the first step toward deciding how much of the work, if any, you can handle by yourself.

**Buy a plan.** Detailed playset plans including full lumber lists are available in books and online for prices ranging from free to hundreds of dollars. The more expensive plans often include some hardware and accessories, and may even offer customer support; the free plans are of varying quality, ranging from up-to-date plans available from lumberyards to reproductions of ancient magazine and book plans. These can be good starting points for a moderately experienced DIYer who can read blueprints and make adjustments as necessary.

**Design and build your own.** If you're an experienced builder and can make scaled drawings, this is the most economical way to go. However, this option will take more time than any of the other options—and this may be just what you're looking for: a fun project for your kids that is a fun project for you to build! With the availability of photos, plans, and how-to information on the Internet, it's not difficult to reverse-engineer features you're not sure about, and accessories like swings and slides always include installation guidelines. Before building, make sure you have up-to-date information about safety features and requirements (see Consumer Product Safety Commission guidelines in the Resources section, page 141).

**You can purchase truly awe-inspiring playsets** that will be the envy of the neighborhood, if you're willing to pay a steep price. Many of these include customizable options.

# Playground Safety

You can choose plastic rather than wood for your playset, or pick swings and a climbing wall instead of a fort, but safety is not a choice. Safety should be the very first thing you think about when considering a playset, and it should lead every decision throughout design, planning, and building. For example, if you plan on building multiple recreation structures in the same backyard, keep at least a 9-foot buffer zone between them. Securely mount play structures to existing framework or anchor them to the ground. And regardless of whether you're building a prefab unit or working from plans you've purchased, always follow manufacturer instructions for all materials. You can ensure the absolute safety of any play structure you install by observing some basic rules when building it.

- Drive nailheads and set screwheads completely into the wood so the heads are flush with the surfaces. Nails or screws that stick out of the wood can pose a serious risk to children. When you've finished building your project, examine it for fasteners that are popping out. Also check for nails or screws that have gone completely through boards and are sticking out the other side. If that happens, clip the end off or grind it down flush with the board.

- Countersink or counterbore holes for anchor bolts so the heads and nuts are recessed.

- Crimp hooks with pliers so sharp edges are not exposed.

- Conduct regular inspections of the structures and look for unusual wear and tear, loose boards or connections, and loose rails. Replace hardware if needed, only with identical hardware.

**A thick bed of mulch** or wood chips such as the base of this playset ensures that any falls result in a soft landing.

## PLAYGROUND SAFETY

For more in-depth information on playground safety, visit the following websites:

- National Program for Playground Safety: www.playgroundsafety.org
- US Consumer Product Safety Commission: www.cpsc.gov/safety-education/safety-guides/playgrounds
- Voice of Play: www.voiceofplay.org/playground-safety

## ARE POST FOOTINGS NECESSARY?

Pouring concrete footings to anchor structural components results in a rock-solid playground, but the process adds hard work and expense. Poured footings are not always necessary, especially if you're building a wide or low structure or using angled supports (like those used for swingsets). Here's a breakdown of the advantages and disadvantages of pouring concrete post footings:

### Advantages
- Creates a stable, permanent base that won't tip or move or sag
- Anchors swingsets and other play equipment solidly
- Makes building on uneven ground easier
- Allows you to make tall, narrow structures and cantilevers without danger of tipping or movement
- Structure can eventually be converted to a storage or garden shed

### Disadvantages
- Adds time and expense to the project, especially if you are building in rocky or hard clay soil
- Structures that can't be moved or disassembled easily may interfere with future landscaping

# Securing Playground Equipment

**Secure the base of any ladders, climbing walls, or ramps.** Any shifting of access structures can cause tumbles from on high, and possible injuries. A great way to anchor ladder bases is with a cleat staked into the ground and attached directly to the ladder.

**Screw-in anchors** help keep playground structures from rocking or tipping, though they can be difficult to install in hard clay or rocky soil. Make sure anchors don't create a tripping hazard.

## SPREAD THE PLAYGROUND MULCH

According to the Consumer Product Safety Commission, about 40,000 children a year visit hospital emergency rooms due to falls from playground equipment. A safe playground will have a cushioning surface, such as mulch or wood chips. Most home playgrounds, however, are located directly on grassy lawns because that is an easy, cost-free surface. However, any grass lawn will become compacted and hard eventually, making falls dangerous. And, of course, you should never build a playground on hard surfaces like concrete or asphalt.

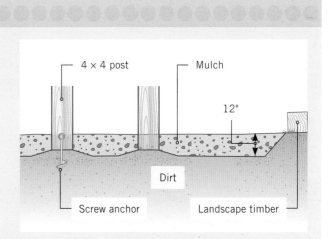

The supports for playground structures need to be anchored on solid, undisturbed ground, so the mulch layer is usually added after the playground is constructed. Once all of the structural elements are anchored, remove some dirt from around the play area—slightly slope the grade away from the supports for the tower and swings. The mulch should extend at least 6' out from all structures and 16' beyond the support beam of a swing. The cushion layer should be installed over landscape fabric to a depth of at least 12". You can reach that depth either by excavating or by adding landscape timbers around the edges to contain the mulch.

# Precut Playground Kit

If you want to design and build a backyard playground that meets your needs, but you don't want to start from scratch, a good option is to buy a precut playground kit. Most home centers and a number of Internet suppliers sell do-it-yourself playground packages containing parts and hardware to make a complete play area. Some of the kits include all of the wood, while others include a list of lumber that you must buy with the set. Dozens of different designs are available, from a basic swingset and slide to elaborate, multilevel play areas with numerous extra features. Most manufacturers design their systems so that optional features can be easily added on.

Most playground systems are designed to be installed with poured concrete footings, but in some cases you may be able to get by with simply anchoring the posts (see page 25). If you choose not to pour footings, it's even more important for the ground underneath the tower and swingset to be very level. To level and smooth the playground area and to stop grass and weeds from growing through it, cut out the sod in the play area, or at least in the area where the structures go, before you begin building.

Some playground kits include all the necessary drill bits and drivers. If your kit doesn't, you'll need a standard selection of spade bits and drill bits, as well as countersink bits for #6 and #8 screws. You'll also need a magnetized Phillips head driver for your drill.

NOTE: The instructions in the following project are intended as a general guide for installing a playground kit that includes precut lumber. The type of playground you purchase may use different materials and techniques than shown here.

**Precut playground packages** contain everything you need except tools. A homeowner with basic skills can put together a play area like this in one or two weekends.

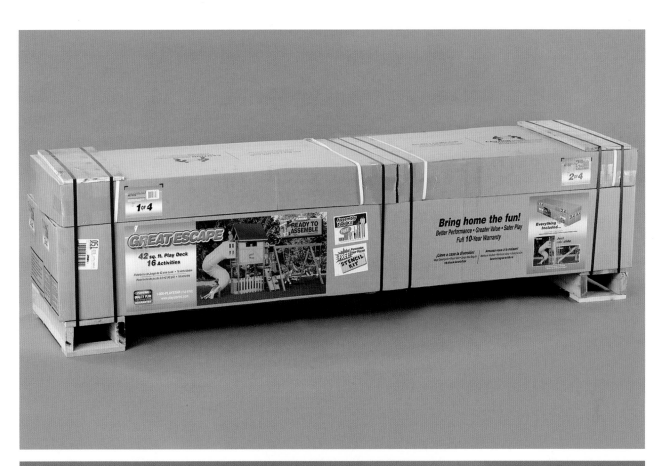

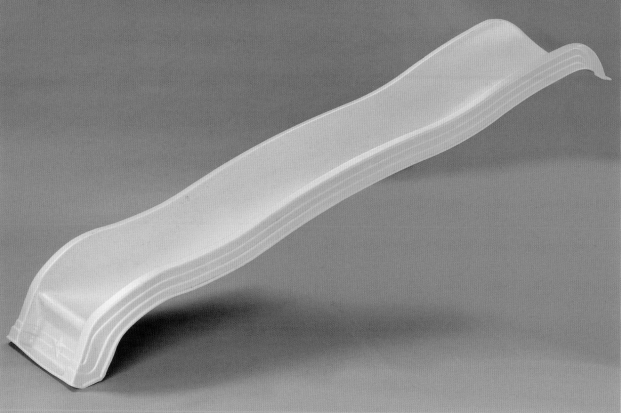

**Playground kits** generally contain all necessary hardware and accessories, and some or all of the wood (top photo). Additional accessories, such as slides, are purchased separately (bottom photo). If you need to purchase additional wood, the kit's shipping carton will show a list of extra lumber required (this will be an extra cost). Playground mulch must also be purchased separately. See page 15 for information about playground mulch.

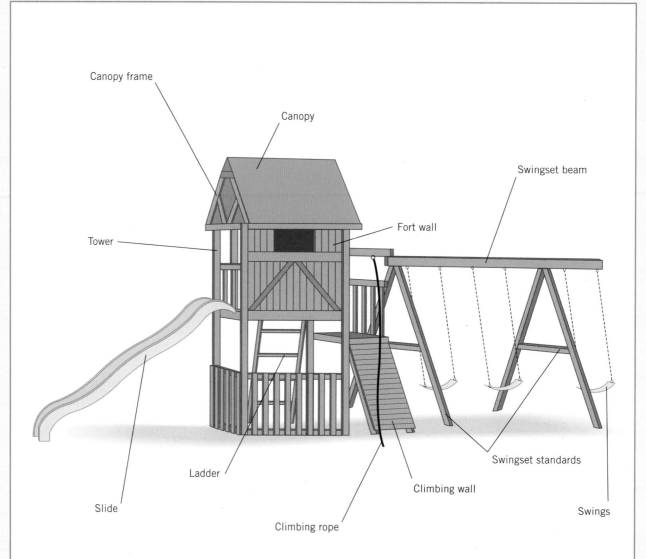

Canopy frame

Canopy

Swingset beam

Tower

Fort wall

Slide

Ladder

Climbing wall

Climbing rope

Swingset standards

Swings

## TOOLS & MATERIALS

Framing square

Carpenter's level

Socket wrench

Adjustable wrench

Drill/driver

Sawhorses

Shovels

Posthole digger
   (if screw-in anchors don't work
   with your soil)

Stakes

Mason's string

Line level

Power saw

Clamps

Ladder

Spacers

Screwdriver

Lag screws

Anchor screws

Playset kit

Eye and ear protection

Work gloves

2 × 6 or 2 × 8

Brackets

Bolts

1½", 2½" deck screws

Tape measure

Swing hangers

1½" panhead screws

Landscape fabric

Mulch

Screw-in anchors

# How to Install a Playground Kit

**Prepare the installation area.** Use strings and stakes to outline the area and then cut out the sod in the play area (buy or rent a sod cutter if you wish to replant the sod elsewhere in your yard). Level the ground. Where possible, level the ground using the lowest spot as a starting point and excavating high areas to that point. Add landscape fabric.

**Begin assembling a tower.** Towers are the principal structural elements in any playground kit. They support slides and other accessories. Generally, they are comprised of fairly simple frames and beams. For the kit shown here, assemble the framework of the tower one side at a time, and then join the sides together on top of flat pieces of 2 × 6 or 2 × 8. Use the drilling template included in the kit as a guide for driving countersunk screws. Locate screws carefully—metal brackets that cover the screwheads are often added later, so the screws have to be positioned carefully. Raise the tower.

**Screw the brackets to the tower frame corners,** making sure that the bolt hole on the long side of the bracket lines up with the centers of the 2 × 4s behind it. Using the large holes in the brackets as guides, drill holes for the bolts. To avoid splintering the back sides, stop drilling as soon as the bit starts to poke through the back, then finish drilling from the other side. Check to make sure everything is still square, and then install and tighten the bolts.

**Install the center joists that connect the platform frames,** fastening them with countersunk 2½" deck screws. Make certain all screwheads are fully seated beneath the wood surface.

*(continued)*

**Install the deckboards with 1½" deck screws** driven into countersunk pilot holes, starting with the two outside pieces. Try to make sure the ends of the deck boards are aligned during installation—clamping a stop block or spacer block to the deck-board support will help align your workpieces. The drainage gaps between the deck boards must be less than ¼".

**Extend the tower walls to the full height** with additional 2 × 4 pieces. Use the drill guide or template (if provided with your kit) to ensure regular alignment of all screws.

**Install the outer framework of 2 × 4s** to support the roof of the playground structure, using corner brackets provided by the kit manufacturer.

**Add additional framing** to strengthen the sides of the tower. The framing on the right will help support the swingset and the climbing bar and climbing wall; the 2 × 4s on the left are used to support the slide.

**Install the bottom railings** and the top back and side railings for the tower structure. Clamp a straight piece of wood on top of (or underneath) the railing at the 1" point to create the setback and to make installation easier. Cut spacers to make the gap even, but check the gap before screwing in the last few boards, just in case, and adjust if necessary.

**Attach railings, siding, and trim.** Install the front railing first, using a ³⁄₁₆" spacer. Then, add the trim pieces. This step is easier if you tilt the structure backwards to the ground—but don't try this without a helper.

**Install the rest of the roof frame.** Use clamps to hold pieces in position before attaching them. Check the center vertical pieces with a carpenter's level to make sure they are plumb.

*(continued)*

**Begin building the swingset.** The swing structure shown here is supported by a pair of angled posts in an A-frame configuration on the end farther from the tower, and a single angled leg on the tower end. Fasten the three legs of the swingset together (they are made with doubled 2 × 4s), and then bolt on the triangular bracket for each leg. Construct the assembly by bolting the triangular brackets together and then screwing on the crosspiece. Add the small brackets to the inside of the crosspiece, with the short legs against the crosspiece (inset). Trim the leg bottoms so they will lie flat on the ground.

**Join the beams and legs.** Screw the 2 × 6 beam pieces to the brackets, making sure the legs are exactly parallel and square to the beam. Drill the ⅜" holes for the bolts using the brackets as a guide. Then screw the second layer of 2 × 6s to the first with 2½" screws.

Swing hanger

**Attach the swing hardware.** First, turn the swing assembly over and place it on sawhorses. Drill guide holes and fasten the sides together with bolts. Drill guide holes for the swing hangers and lag screws and install them so that the moving hanger swings perpendicular to the beam.

**Add the swingset to the tower.** Lift the swingset into place and fasten it to the tower with a bolt through the swing beam and a 2 × 4 crosspiece near the base fastened with metal angles and bolts.

**Installing the climbing wall.** Attach the climbing wall supports to the tower frame with the provided brackets. The ends of the supports are angle-cut at the top and the bottom. Attach the top and bottom crossboards to the outer supports and then center the middle support board and attach it by driving deck screws through the crossboards and into the support.

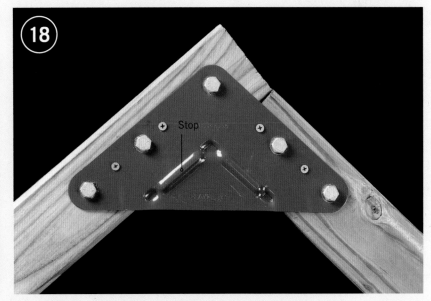

Stop

**Add the remaining crossboards** in the climbing wall, working down from the top and making sure the boards are fitted tightly together.

**Start building the climbing bar assembly.** The climbing bars function as a ladder that is mounted to the tower on the side opposite from the climbing wall. Assemble the climbing bar standards with four triangular metal brackets included with the kit. The stops on the sides of the brackets that contact the standard will set the correct angle for the standards if the boards are tight against the stops. *(continued)*

**Attach the climbing bars to the standards,** making sure the standards are parallel and oriented correctly. Use 1½" panhead screws to attach the bars at 12" intervals on the bottom leg and at 10¾" intervals along the top (or as directed by the instructions for your kit).

**Connect the climbing bar to the tower.** First, dig holes into the play surface at the correct locations for the legs of the climbing bar standards. Set the legs into the 2"-deep holes (inset), and then fasten the top ends of the standards to the tower with brackets and lag screws.

**Anchor all sides of the swingset,** along with the climbing bar and climbing wall, using screw-in anchors (see page 25). If the anchors don't work properly in your soil type, dig a 2'-deep posthole, fill it with concrete, and set the anchor in that. Bolt the anchor to the structure with ⅜ × 1½" lag screws.

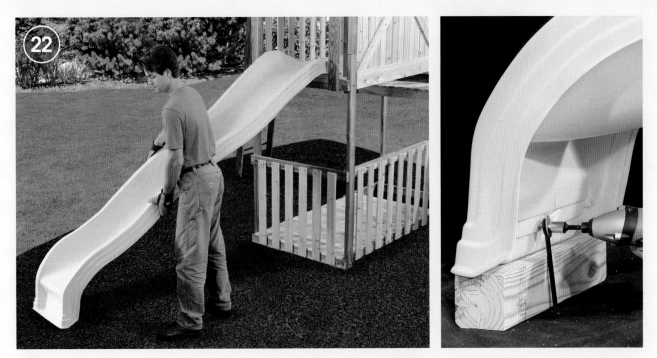

**Attach the slide.** First, position the slide (left photo) and then attach it to the tower at the top with fasteners as provided (or recommended) by the manufacturer. Then, bolt the slide at the base to a screw-in anchor.

**TIP:** Attach the bottom of the slide to a 4 × 4 spacer and then attach the spacer to a screw-in anchor (right photo). This provides a solid footing for the slide while raising it so the bottom is not completely covered by groundcover or mulch.

**Add other accessories,** including swings, the roof, and the climbing rope. You'll need to drill access holes for the climbing rope in the climbing wall. Add approved groundcover (see page 15).

# DIY Playset

If you want a playset, designing and building your own from scratch is not as easy or fast as buying a precut system, but if you have the tools and know-how you can save money and create a more unique and imaginative playset by doing it yourself.

The simplest way to get started is to design and build the playground in separate parts, beginning with a simple, rectangular platform. You can then add slides, a swingset, a climbing rope, and other features as your time and budget allow. Before you start, mark the area where the play structure will go in your yard, then add additional area for playground mulch (at least 6 feet out in all directions). Cut away the sod in this area and level the ground—preferably by digging out soil instead of filling in, since fill will continue to compress even after it is compacted.

## PLAYSET HARDWARE

Although it's a little more work initially, the best way to make sure your playground will be solid and stable is to pour concrete footings and anchor the platform posts to the footings. Ideally, the footings should extend below the frostline (check with your local building department if you do not know your frostline depth). If you pour concrete footings, make sure that the concrete is covered by several inches of dirt or playground mulch to prevent injuries.

When building your playset, you can set the posts into postholes, add a few inches of gravel, and then fill the hole with concrete, or you can set the posts into exterior-rated metal post bases that are anchored to the concrete.

**NOTE:** Metal post bases are designed to work in groups and are not a good choice for single posts or even post pairs. They do not provide sufficient side-to-side rigidity.

If your structure is very wide or low to the ground, you can forego footings and instead bolt the posts to a framework of 2 × 6s (or larger), which will spread the weight over a large area and keep the platform stable. If you attach a swing or cantilevered beam to the platform, use one of these methods to hold the structure in place: fasten long screw anchors at the corners; attach structure to concrete footings; or weigh the structure down with an attached sandbox.

**Hardware and equipment** specially designed for playgrounds can be purchased in kits or as needed. In addition to saving time, using engineered hardware is a safe method for designing critical joinery. For example, if you are wondering how many lag bolts you need to make a post/beam connection on a swingset, you'll find the easiest answer is zero if you purchase an engineered A-frame bracket instead. A-frame bracket (A), screw-in anchors (B), swing hardware (C), swing chain and seat (D), galvanized joist hangers and brackets (E), hot-dipped galvanized fasteners (F), hot-dipped galvanized eye bolt (G).

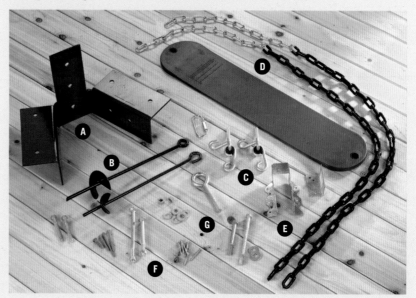

**Save money** by designing and building your own play structure using standard building materials and your own ingenuity.

## MATERIALS

(4) 4 × 4" post bases

(4) 8"-dia. × 2' tube forms

Concrete

Landscape fabric

(1) 1 × 3" × 8'

(1 lb.) 2" deck screws

(2 lb.) 2½" deck screws

(44) ⅜ × 5" carriage bolts,
   washers, nuts

Joist hanger brackets and nails

(8) 2¾" metal corners

(2) 1¼ × 8⅝ × 3⁹⁄₁₆" U-shaped
   metal straps

(6) ⅜ × 6" carriage bolts,
   washers, nuts

(1) ⅜ × 5" eyebolt with washer,
   lock washer, nut

18' ¾"-dia. rope

Metal thimble for rope

Lumber (see below)

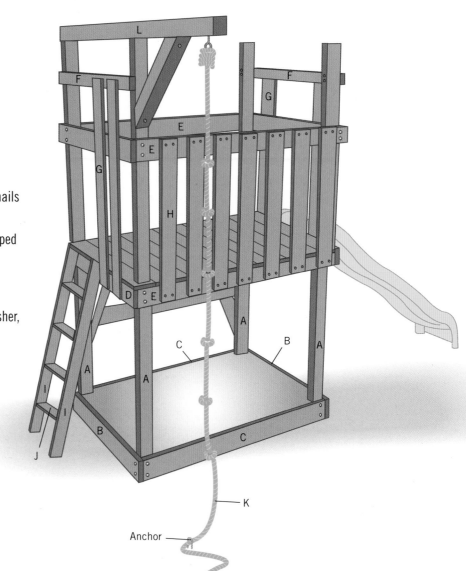

## CUTTING LIST

| KEY | NO. | DIMENSION | MATERIAL |
|-----|-----|-----------|----------|
| **BASE & PLATFORM** | | | |
| A | 4 | 3½ × 3½ × 10' | Pine (PT) |
| B | 2 | 1½ × 7¼ × 51" | " |
| C | 2 | 1½ × 7¼ × 69" | " |
| D | 4 | 1½ × 5½ × 51" | " |
| E | 4 | 1½ × 5½ × 58" | " |
| F | 2 | 1½ × 3½ × 48" | " |
| G | 4 | 5/4 × 5½ × 58" | Decking (PT) |
| H | 14 | 5/4 × 5½ × 42" | Decking (PT) |

| KEY | NO. | DIMENSION | MATERIAL |
|-----|-----|-----------|----------|
| **LADDER** | | | |
| I | 2 | 1½ × 3½ × 61½" | Pine (PT) |
| J | 4 | 1½ × 3½ × 17" | " |
| **CLIMBING ROPE** | | | |
| K | 1 | 3½ × 3½ × 7' | Pine (PT) |
| L | 1 | 3½ × 3½ × 30" | " |

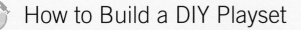

# How to Build a DIY Playset

**Lay out the project area,** including the required excavation of surface materials for the buffer zone around the playset. Use batterboards and mason's string to outline the area, making sure the corners are square. Tie a second set of strings to the squared layout strings so they intersect directly over the centers of the post locations.

**Mark digging points** on the ground directly below post locations. Untie the mason's strings.

**NOTE:** Contact your local utilities company to have them mark buried gas, plumbing, or electrical lines before you start digging.

**Dig holes for concrete footings** using a posthole digger or a power auger. Where feasible, dig at least a few inches past the frostline for your area.

**Fill the forms with concrete,** tie the mason's string back onto the batterboards and level them, and then set J-bolts into the concrete directly beneath the centers of the planned post locations. *(continued)*

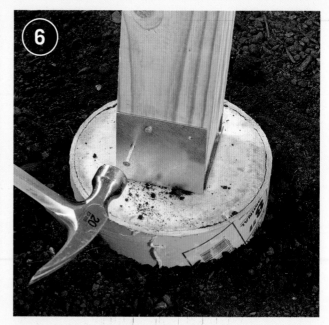

Set the metal post bases and washers over the bolts and hand-tighten the nuts (a standoff base is designed to elevate the post bottom to eliminate ground contact while still holding the post securely). Leave one side of the post base open so you have access with an open-end wrench to tighten each nut after trimming and aligning the post tops.

Fasten the bottoms of the posts to the standoff hardware with 10d galvanized nails, joist hanger nails or other fasteners as specified by the post base manufacturer. All predrilled guide holes in the hardware should be filled with a fastener. Plumb and brace the posts.

NOTE: The tops of the 4 × 4 posts should be high enough that they can all be trimmed back to final height later.

Temporary brace

Attach 2 × 6 pressure-treated frame boards to the posts so the bottoms are level with one another and slightly above grade. Cut the 2 × 6s so they form a complete frame around the posts once installed. Use clamps and deck screws to tack the members in place until they are leveled and located exactly where you want them. After drilling the bolt guide holes, use a 1¼" spade bit to counterbore ½"-deep holes. Wrap masking tape around the spade bit to mark the ½" depth.

Install landscape fabric. To prevent weeds and grass from growing through the sand, spread landscape fabric over the ground inside the structure area and staple it to the inside surfaces of the 2 × 6 frame. Hold the top of the fabric back about 3" from the tops of the frame boards. For extra holding power, use thin wood strips as retainers for stapling or nailing the fabric.

**Attach the platform side boards** so the tops are approximately 59" above grade. First, tack the side boards to the 4 × 4 posts with a 2½" deck screw at each end. Make sure the sides and all other members are level and plumb and then drill two bolt holes at each end for ⅜ × 5" carriage bolts. The end of each hole that will receive the nut and washer should have a 1¼"-dia. × ½" deep counterbore. Do not counterbore for carriage bolt heads. Tighten nuts onto the carriage bolts with a socket wrench or impact driver.

**Trim post tops.** Identify the post with the lowest post base and measure up on that post to the finished post height for the project. Mark the height and then use a laser level (or a straight board with a carpenter's level attached to it) to transfer the post top height to the other posts. After the frame and platform are installed, trim the posts along the lines. A cordless circular saw is a good tool for trimming post tops.

**Add the platform support joists,** using joist hanger hardware to support the 2 × 6 joist material between the side boards. Space the joists equally. The tops of the joists should be flush with the tops of the side boards.

*(continued)*

**Cut pieces of 5/4 decking** (actual thickness is 1") for the platform and install them with deck screws driven into the support joists. Arrange the boards on the joist supports first and adjust them so the gaps between boards are equal, consistent, and do not exceed ¼". Drive screws in a regular pattern, as the screwheads will be visible.

**Fasten 2 × 6 railings to the posts** on the sides of the structure, using ⅜ × 5" carriage bolts. The tops of the railings should be 8' above ground. Counterbore the posts so the nuts and washers are recessed. Also install 2 × 4 railings on the other two sides (narrow sides) at 111" high. Paint or stain the playset with exterior-grade paint if desired.

## ⚠ SAFETY TIP

**For safety,** add wide balusters made from deck boards to the sides. The gaps between boards should not exceed 3". Leave openings for ladders, slides, and any other accessories you wish to attach.

**Fill the framed base enclosure with sand** to create a sandbox (or use mulch or pea gravel, if you prefer).

# How to Build a Ladder

**Measure and cut the ladder standards** from a pressure-treated 2 × 4. Look for tight-grained lumber with no visible defects. The steps are set at a 15° angle so they'll be level when the angled standards are set on flat ground. The back edges of the standards at the top are cut at a 75° angle.

15°

**A wooden ladder** provides easy, safe access up into the fort portion of your project. This ladder is sturdy and simple to build. You'll need: (2) 2 × 4 × 61½", (4) 2 × 4 × 17", (1) 2 × 4 × 24", and (8) 2¾" metal corners.

Box

**Attach the steps.** Nail one plate of each metal corner brace to the ladder sides at the correct spacing (the steps generally are 12" apart on-center) and then nail the bracket to the underside of the step using joist hanger nails.

**Attach a ladder base** to the bottom of the ladder to function as a spreader. Screw the 24"-long base to the bottoms of the ladder sides with deck screws, then set the ladder in place on a bed of gravel. Secure the ladder to the playset deck through the back with two deck screws per side driven into the frame.

# How to Attach a Slide

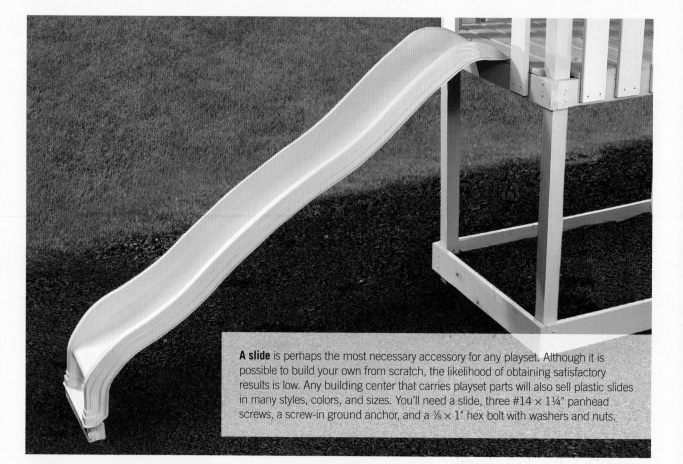

**A slide** is perhaps the most necessary accessory for any playset. Although it is possible to build your own from scratch, the likelihood of obtaining satisfactory results is low. Any building center that carries playset parts will also sell plastic slides in many styles, colors, and sizes. You'll need a slide, three #14 × 1¼" panhead screws, a screw-in ground anchor, and a ⅜ × 1" hex bolt with washers and nuts.

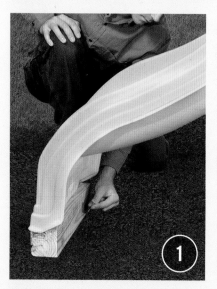

**Mark the slide anchor location** onto the ground using a cap nail. When using a thick bed of playground mulch, raise the bottom of the slide by attaching it to a 4 × 4. This 60" slide is secured to the playset tower so the top edge is 60" above ground. To attach the slide temporarily, drive #14 × 1¼" panhead screws through the screw holes in the slide lip.

**Drive an anchor for the slide base** into the ground, after removing the slide, at the post marked in Step 1. The eye hook at the top should be aligned with the bolt hole in the slide.

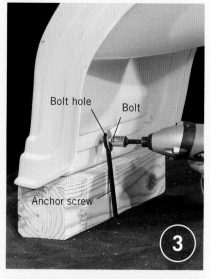

Bolt hole    Bolt

Anchor screw

**Reinstall the slide,** driving the fasteners through the top lip and into the playset structure. Use an exterior bolt (⅜ × 1" is used here) to attach the base of the slide to the anchor you've driven for it. The base should be resting on solid ground (not on mulch or other loose materials) or a spacer, as shown.

# How to Add a Climbing Rope

A climbing rope can be attached to a cantilevered support beam that is securely affixed to the top of your play structure.

**(1)**

**Attach a 7'-long 4 × 4** to the top of the playset structure to support a climbing rope. Use joist hanger nails and U-shaped metal straps or long metal straps to fasten the cantilevered 4 × 4 to the post tops.

**(2)**

**Add a 4 × 4 brace** with a 45° angle cut at each end. The brace is attached with a ⅜ × 6" bolt at each end and reinforced with the same U-shaped strap hardware used to attach the beam.

**(3)**

**Hang the climbing rope.** A ⅜ × 5" eyebolt can be attached to the cantilevered end of the beam, about 6" in, for an easy tie-off point. You can purchase fancier hardware, such as a swivel hook. Tie knots every foot or so in the rope for better gripping while climbing.

**(4)**

**Anchor the bottom of the rope** to a screw-in anchor or a board that's bolted to the base of the fort. The rope should not hang loose for safety reasons. If you are tying the rope to a screw-in anchor, use a large enough knot to cover the top of the anchor screw eye.

# DIY Swingset

Swingsets are the most popular and common playground feature, and for good reason. There is something eternally pleasing about the simple back-and-forth rhythm of a swing in motion. It's relaxing, enjoyable, and entertaining (even for adult kids). That's why a backyard swingset is an absolute must-have for any home with children.

Stability is priority number one when it comes to building a swingset. The joints must be secured for safety and longevity—something that is achieved in this structure using special A-frame brackets, and 2 × 6 cross braces. To ensure absolute stability, each leg should be anchored in place to solid ground, not just set on top of loose infill.

**Swings are virtually a requirement in any playset.** This swingset is bolted to a DIY playset, but it can easily be modified into a freestanding swinging structure.

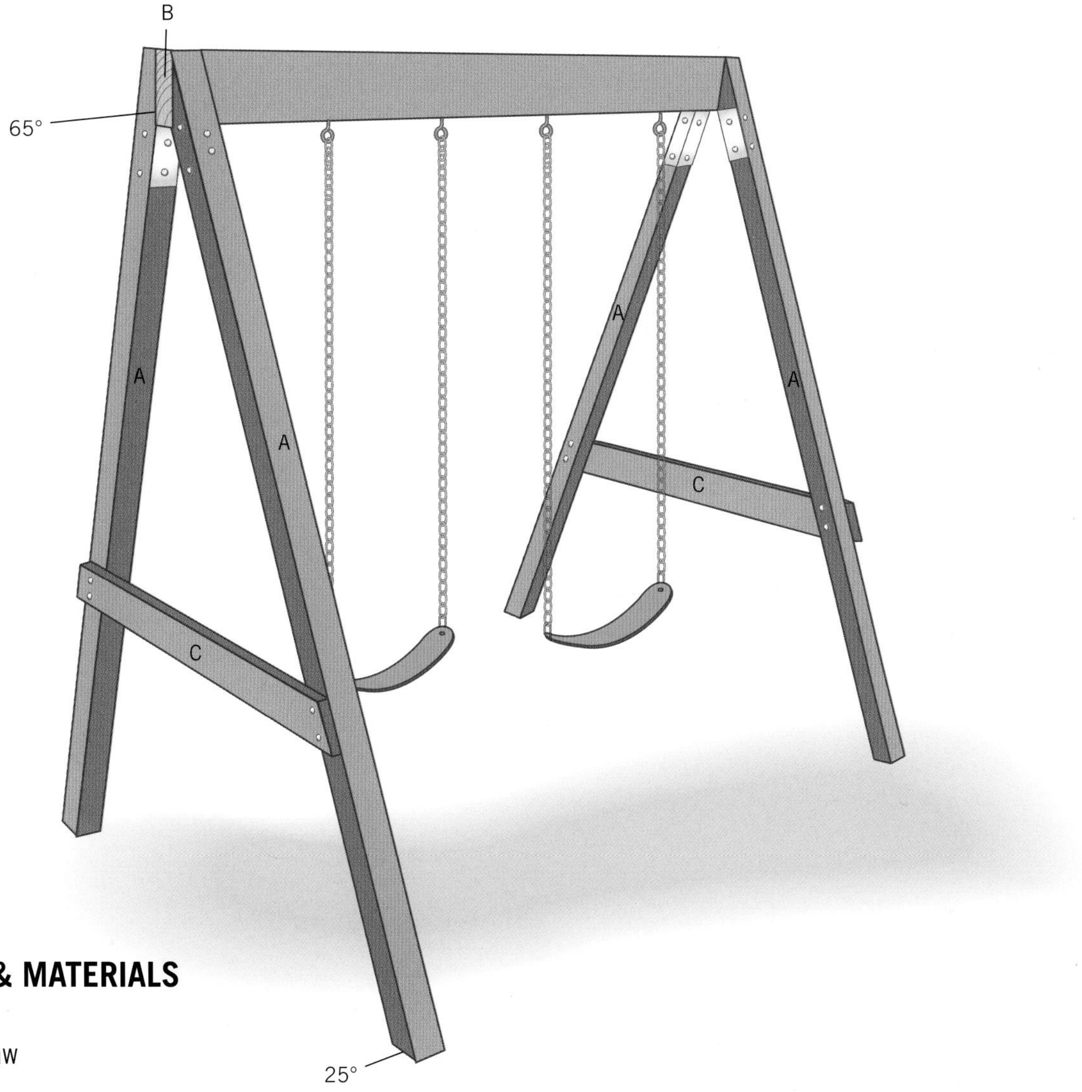

B

65°

A

A

A

A

C

C

25°

## TOOLS & MATERIALS
Pencil

Circular saw

Protractor

Power miter saw

Drill/driver

Spade bit

Sawhorses

Clamps

Stepladder

Eye and ear protection

Work gloves

(8) $\frac{3}{8} \times 5$" carriage bolts, nuts, washers

(2) $\frac{3}{8} \times 6$" carriage bolts, nuts, washers

(2) Swingworks A-frame brackets
    (see Resources, page 141)

Swing seats, chains, and hardware

## CUTTING LIST

| KEY | NO. | DIMENSION | MATERIAL |
|-----|-----|-----------|----------|
| A | 4 | $3\frac{1}{2} \times 3\frac{1}{2} \times 104$" | Pine (PT) |
| B | 1 | $3\frac{1}{2} \times 5\frac{1}{2} \times 8$' | " |
| C | 2 | $1\frac{1}{2} \times 5\frac{1}{2} \times 6$' | " |

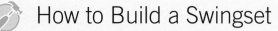

**Mark the posts for cutting.** If you are using A-frame brackets (strongly recommended), purchase the hardware beforehand and mark the posts using the A-frame bracket as a guide. If you are not using brackets, use a protractor or a speed square as a gauge to mark the tops of the posts at around 65° so they will meet to form a stable A-shaped structure with sufficient leg spread.

**Cut the long angles on each post with a circular saw,** then square off the top edge with a power miter saw or circular saw.

**Bolt the A-frame brackets onto the 4 × 6,** and then predrill the holes for the eye bolts that hold the swing. Use a long spade bit for the holes.

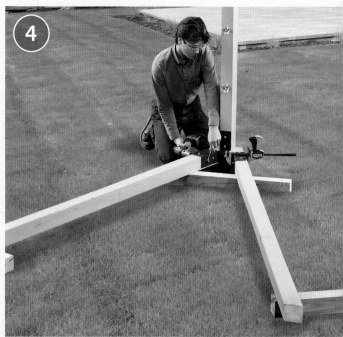

**Assemble the legs.** Lay the 4 × 4 legs for one side on a flat area, set the 4 × 6 on top of them, and then bolt the legs to the brackets. Use the fasteners recommended by the hardware manufacturer. You'll need a helper to hold the 4 × 6 steady.

**Attach the second leg.** Use a stepladder or helpers to hold the 4 × 4s steady and in place as you finish bolting into the brackets.

**Clamp the 2 × 6 ties in position.** Drill the bolt holes, and then counterbore the holes on the inside. Bolt the 2 × 6 on with 5" carriage bolts.

**Anchor the swingset.** Tack the swingset structure in place against the platform of the adjoining playset. Using a long drill bit, drill through each 4 × 4 leg and bolt the swing to the platform.

**Hang the swings** using the mounting hardware and chains or rope supplied with or recommended by the manufacturer. Test to make sure the ground clearance is adequate and adjust as necessary.

# Backyard Fun

E ven small backyards have room for a wide variety of play structures and projects, from elaborate playhouses to simple water slides. Most of the projects in this chapter are based on traditional play—modern variations of what kids (and even grownups) have been doing for fun out in the backyard for centuries. Most of them don't have to cost a lot of money either—even the more elaborate projects can be downsized or simplified.

Some of the projects in this chapter are for small children, some are primarily for older children, and some can be enjoyed by all ages. As with any project, keep safety in mind. Counterbore or bury all protruding bolts and screws, round over sharp edges, and inspect your work for places where clothes or body parts can get trapped or snagged. Apply mulch or another shock-absorbent material anywhere there's a chance of falling, because sooner or later someone will. And remember to inspect the project occasionally after it's up and in use. Bolts can loosen over time as the wood dries out and may need retightening; wood can crack and warp as it ages, creating sharp splinters; and pieces may break or come loose due to hard use.

## In this chapter:
- Timberframe Sandbox
- Seesaw
- Zipline
- Classic Tree Swing
- Jungle Gym
- Obstacle Course
- Swinging Rope Challenge

# Timberframe Sandbox

## TOOLS & MATERIALS

(14) 4 × 4" × 8' cedar

(1) 1 × 8" × 12' cedar

(2) 1 × 6" × 8' cedar

(2) 2 × 2" × 6' cedar

Coarse gravel

Sand

Wood sealer/protectant

Heavy-duty plastic sheeting
or landscape fabric

2" galvanized screws

6" galvanized barn nails
or landscape spikes

Pavers (optional)

Child-safe friction hinges

Eye and ear protection

Work gloves

Building this sandbox requires a good deal more effort than if you simply nailed four boards together and dumped a pile of sand in the middle. The timber construction is both charming and solid. A storage box at one end gives kids a convenient place to keep their toys. The opposite end has built-in seats, allowing children to sit above the sand as they play.

The gravel bed and landscape fabric provide a nice base for the sandbox, allowing water to drain while keeping weeds from sprouting in the sand. The gravel and liner also keep sand from migrating out of the box. The structure is set into the ground for stability and to keep the top of the pavers at ground level so you can easily mow around them. When your children outgrow the sandbox, you can turn it into a raised garden bed.

**If you have small children,** a backyard just isn't complete without a sandbox. This version is nicely sized, sturdy, and designed for ease of cleaning.

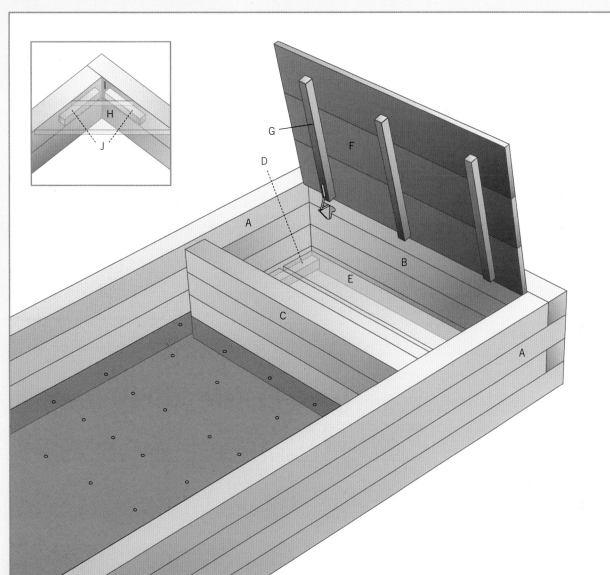

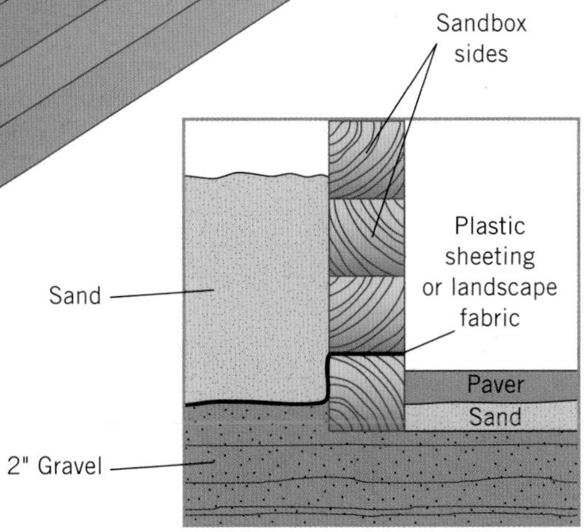

## CUTTING LIST

| KEY | PART | NO. | DIMENSION | MATERIAL |
|-----|------|-----|-----------|----------|
| A | Sandbox sides | 8 | 3½ × 3½ × 92½" | Ext. lumber |
| B | Sandbox ends | 8 | 3½ × 3½ × 44½" | Ext. lumber |
| C | Storage box wall | 4 | 3½ × 3½ × 41" | Ext. lumber |
| D | Floor cleats | 2 | 1½ × 1½ × 18" | Ext. lumber |
| E | Floorboards | 3 | ¾ × 5½ × 41" | Ext. lumber |
| F | Lid boards | 3 | ¾ × 7½ × 40½" | Ext. lumber |
| G | Lid cleats | 3 | 1½ × 1½ × 18" | Ext. lumber |
| H | Bench boards | 2 | ¾ × 5½ × 18" | Ext. lumber |
| I | Corner bench boards | 2 | ¾ × 5½ × 7" | Ext. lumber |
| J | Bench cleats | 4 | 1½ × 1½ × 10" | Ext. lumber |

Sandbox sides

Plastic sheeting or landscape fabric

Sand

Paver

Sand

2" Gravel

# How to Build a Timberframe Sandbox

## TIMBERFRAME SANDBOX PREP

Although the construction details of this simple rectangular sandbox are important, the longevity and aesthetic value depend just as much on proper site and material preparation. Cut the timbers with a circular saw, coat them with wood sealer, and let them dry completely before building the box. Cut the storage floor cleats and flooring to length. Cut the seat 2 × 2" seat cleats and lid cleats. Cut the lid boards to length. Clip the seat boards with a 45° end cut and save the cut piece. Set up a staging area with all the tools, hardware, lumber, and plastic tarp on which to place the sod you remove from the sandbox trench. Mark the 48 × 96" excavation area outline with lime or landscaping paint. Use this outline to guide positioning stakes at each corner, and strings for the outline.

**Use a spade or shovel** to remove the sod inside the area, then dig a trench 2" deep by 4" wide around the perimeter inside the border. Place side and end timbers in the trench and use a level at the corners to ensure the timbers are level. Drill two ³⁄₁₆" pilot holes through the sides and drive 6" barn nails through the holes.

**For the storage box,** measure and mark in from one end 18" on each side. Align the box wall timber and score the soil on either side of it. Remove the timber and dig a 3"-deep trench for the wall timber so that it sits ½" lower than the rest of the frame. Drill ¹⁄₁₆" pilot holes and fasten the frame to the wall ends with 6" barn nails. Fill the sandbox portion with 2" gravel, tamp it down, and cover with perforated plastic sheet.

**Place a second level of timbers over the first,** sandwiching the plastic sheet and staggering the timber joints with the bottom joints. Drill pilot holes every 24" down into the first layer and fasten the layers together with 6" galvanized barn nails. Repeat with the remaining layers, then build up the timber wall, fastening the additional layers as before. Trim the excess sheeting with a utility knife.

**Screw the storage floor cleats to the sides** with 2" galvanized screws. Screw the floorboards to the cleats, leaving ½" gaps for drainage. Lay the lid boards side by side and position lid cleats on each side and in the middle. Drill pilot holes and use 2" galvanized screws to fasten the cleats in place. Attach the lid to the frame with the hinges.

**Measure and mark** ¾" down from the top of the sandbox at two corners. Align the top edge of the bench cleats with the marks and screw them to the frame. Screw the clipped corners of the bench board into the corner of the frame on the cleats. Butt the seat to the clipped triangle and fasten the seat to the cleats. Repeat with the second seat.

**Fill the sandbox with sand** 4" from the top. Mark an area for the pavers around the sandbox, then remove sod and soil to a depth of the pavers plus 2". Spread a 2" layer of sand, then smooth and tamp. Set the pavers in place using a level or straightedge to ensure they are even and flush. Set the pavers by tapping them with a rubber mallet. Fill gaps between pavers with sand, then spray with water.

# Seesaw

## TOOLS & MATERIALS

| | |
|---|---|
| Premixed concrete | Pipe joint compound |
| Gravel | Handles (conduit fittings) |
| Lumber | $3/8 \times 8"$ galvanized |
| Mulch | carriage bolts with |
| Exterior wood glue | nuts and washers |
| Circular saw | Galvanized pipe & fittings |
| Pipe wrench | Eye and ear protection |
| Level | Work gloves |
| Sandpaper | Protective finish |

For kids, the seesaw (also called a teeter-totter) is both enjoyable recreation and a good introduction to simple machines and basic physics. It's a revelation for a child to be able to lift a huge grownup off the ground just by having them sit closer to the pivot point.

A seesaw can be as basic as a board laid across a log, or it may be an elaborate wooden construction perfectly balanced on a pivot point that rotates in any direction while going up and down. If you design your own seesaw, experiment with it on graph paper before building it. Draw different combinations of pivot point heights and board lengths; then see what happens when the board goes down. Small changes in height and length can mean the difference between a 3-foot drop and a 6-foot drop, changing a gentle kid-friendly seesaw into a seesaw that terrifies (or thrills) adults.

Make sure the pivot point is solid, either by building a wide, stable base or by embedding the supporting posts in at least 2 feet of concrete. Lock the seesaw board onto the pipe or dowel that it pivots on ( for example, with pipe strap)—otherwise it can bounce off the pipe.

**Whether you call it a seesaw** or a teeter-totter, this venerable plaything has been a fixture for thousands of years, and almost every culture has developed a version of it. All you need to make one is a long board with handles and a center pivot.

# SEESAW

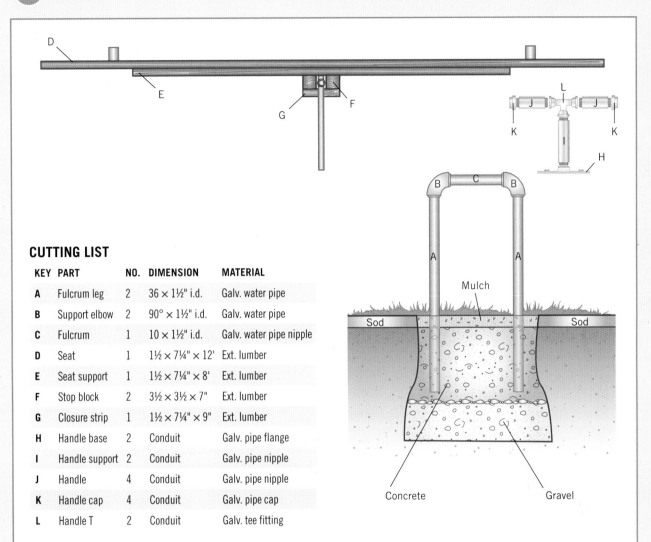

## CUTTING LIST

| KEY | PART | NO. | DIMENSION | MATERIAL |
|-----|------|-----|-----------|----------|
| A | Fulcrum leg | 2 | 36 × 1½" i.d. | Galv. water pipe |
| B | Support elbow | 2 | 90° × 1½" i.d. | Galv. water pipe |
| C | Fulcrum | 1 | 10 × 1½" i.d. | Galv. water pipe nipple |
| D | Seat | 1 | 1½ × 7¼" × 12' | Ext. lumber |
| E | Seat support | 1 | 1½ × 7¼" × 8' | Ext. lumber |
| F | Stop block | 2 | 3½ × 3½ × 7" | Ext. lumber |
| G | Closure strip | 1 | 1½ × 7¼" × 9" | Ext. lumber |
| H | Handle base | 2 | Conduit | Galv. pipe flange |
| I | Handle support | 2 | Conduit | Galv. pipe nipple |
| J | Handle | 4 | Conduit | Galv. pipe nipple |
| K | Handle cap | 4 | Conduit | Galv. pipe cap |
| L | Handle T | 2 | Conduit | Galv. tee fitting |

**A wide, stable base** allows you to set up this seesaw on any level area. Seesaws large enough to be used by several children at a time are available from online suppliers, and can be assembled with standard hand tools.

## ORDER A SEESAW ONLINE

If you're not sure you want to build your own seesaw, or if you want a seesaw that's not fixed in place, many other models are available from retailers and online suppliers. (See Resources on page 141, or just search for Seesaws.)

Different online suppliers sell different components. Some sell plans alone, along with shopping lists that will guide you to what you need from any home center. Other suppliers provide kits with hardware, instructions, and even toll-free numbers to call if you need to ask questions. A few companies offer turnkey seesaw kits with all the pre-cut and prefinished lumber, hardware, and detailed instructions included. The more the supplier offers, the more expensive the kit will be.

# How to Build a Seesaw

**Build the fulcrum assembly** from 1½" (inside diameter) galvanized steel water pipe. Tighten a pair of 90° elbows to the threaded ends of a 10" nipple. Use a pipe wrench to crank them at least a full turn past hand-tight. Use pipe joint compound or Teflon tape to lubricate the threads so you can tighten the fitting more easily. Add a 36" section of galvanized pipe to the open end of each elbow.

**Set the fulcrum assembly into concrete.** Build a 2 × 4 brace to support the assembly while the concrete hardens. The ends of the fulcrum legs should extend 14" into the concrete, making the top of the assembly approximately 24" above grade. After digging the hole for the fulcrum, widen the base on all sides to create a bell shape for extra stability.

**Pour concrete into the hole.** Add 2 to 4" of drainage gravel (such as 1-2" river rock) to the bottom of the hole before pouring the concrete. Smooth the concrete surface with a trowel, forming a crown so water doesn't collect.

**4**

**Make the seesaw board.** The seesaw board is created from a pair of 2 × 8s that are fastened together face-to face with construction adhesive and screws. Glue and screw the 2 × 8s together, then mark the center and outside diameter of the pipe on the bottom board.

**5**

**Glue and bolt 4 × 4 stop blocks** to the seesaw board so they fit around both sides of the pipe, which should fit snugly between the blocks. Use two 3⁄8 × 8" carriage bolts for each side, making sure the bolt head is on the top (longer) 2 × 8 and the bolt is fastened on the bottom side (shorter).

**Place the seesaw board** onto the pipe at the top of the fulcrum assembly. Then attach a wood closure strip beneath the fulcrum bar to lock the seatboard in position.

**6**

**7**

**Apply the finishing touches.** Sand the boards using up to 150-grit sandpaper for a smooth finish that will resist splintering. You may make small arched cutouts on both edges near the seatboard ends if you wish to create a classic seesaw detail. Attach a sturdy handle 18 to 24" from each end. Use very large door pulls or custom-make the handles—the ones seen here are made by fabricating rigid conduit and fittings into a T-shape. Apply a protective finish (clear sealer or paint) to all wood surfaces. Occasionally lubricate the top bar in the fulcrum with graphite spray to improve performance and decrease noise.

# Zipline

## TOOLS & MATERIALS

| | |
|---|---|
| (2) Metal thimbles for cable | Drill with spade bits and bit extender |
| (6) Stainless-steel cable clamps | Heavy-duty, exterior-rated eyebolts, washers, and nuts |
| Discarded tire | |
| ¾" turnbuckle | Zipline kit |
| Mulch | Eye and ear protection |
| Stepladder | Work gloves |
| Rubber mallet | |

A zipline is a simple contraption consisting of a seat or handle hanging from a heavy-duty pulley that is suspended from a steel cable. The cable is tied between a pair of trees, posts, or other sturdy structures you can find or build—as long as one is higher than the other. If you're starting the cable from a treehouse or platform, make sure any framing that the eyebolt attaches to is rock-solid.

A zipline can be slow, gentle, and close enough to the ground to push off and stop yourself with your feet. Or, it can be very high and very fast, carrying you down mountainsides or across lakes, rivers, and canyons. The longest known zipline is 1.2 miles, drops almost 1,000 feet, and reaches speeds of up to 100 miles per hour. These "extreme" ziplines should be created by professionals only and used under the supervision of a qualified professional.

You can create a smaller, safer version of that mind-bending ride in your own backyard with a length of steel cable, some long eyebolts, and a zipline kit with a heavy-duty tandem pulley. Do not use the standard pulleys sold at hardware stores for ziplines—they're not meant for this application. Similarly, use only braided cable (usually stainless steel) that has been specifically selected and packaged for a zipline. You'll find a number of purveyors of zipline products on the Internet (see Resources, page 141).

## SAFETY

The minimum safety equipment for any backyard zipline is a harness, helmet, and gloves. You may also want to add knee and elbow pads. Ziplines should always be used with adult supervision, and an adult should test out any new zipline before kids use it. When deciding a zipline kit to buy, check the US Consumer Product Safety Commission website (www.cpsc.gov) for any current or recent recalls. Make sure the zipline course runs over soft bushes or infill, such as mulch.

**Safe usage of any zipline** requires safety equipment and adults should always test out the zipline before kids use it.

**A kit and a few basic tools** are all you need to install a zipline. Be sure to buy heavy-duty stainless-steel or galvanized fittings (kits are available from online suppliers). Always check online reviews of zipline kits, and check the Consumer Product Safety Commission website for any information about the kit you're considering.

## ZIPLINE REQUIREMENTS

For a good ride, make the zipline at least 75' long, with a minimum slope of 5'. Trees must be heathy and at least 10" in diameter. If you're starting at a treehouse or platform, reinforce the framing with additional fasteners or metal brackets.

Test the run before drilling the holes. Wrap the cable around the trees, secure it with cable clamps and hold it in position at the level where the eyebolt will be attached with wood clamps or large nails. Then tie a heavy sandbag to the handle so it's hanging where a person would be and send it down the cable. If it seems too slow or fast, move one end of the cable to compensate. Watch for obstacles in the path of the cable, and cut branches back 4' on all sides.

Lighter-duty zipline kits made for use by children are sold in relatively inexpensive kits (always do your homework to investigate customer ratings and reviews of any zipline product). The maximum distances of these kits is usually about 90'. Shorter is usually safer. A high-adventure zipline requires a very unusual backyard with tall trees and ample space. But setting up a slightly tamer run from your deck to the old maple tree is a great way for people of all ages to learn and develop skills.

# How to Install a Zipline

**Drill a hole through the center of each tree** (high end and low end) for an eyebolt. The holes should be the same diameter as the eyebolt shaft. You'll need to use an extra-long spade bit or a bit extender to clear a tree trunk, which should be at least 10" in diameter.

**Insert an eyebolt** (stainless-steel or triple-dipped galvanized) through the guide hole and then secure it to the tree with a wide washer, such as a fender washer, and a nut. The end of the bolt should protrude 1 to 2" past the tree. Inspect the nut periodically to make sure it is still tight.

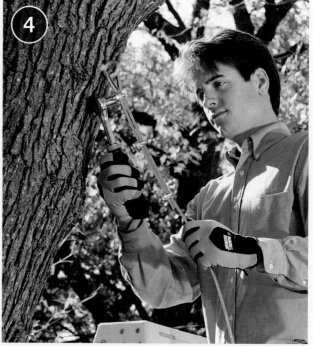

**Attach a turnbuckle to the eyebolt** on the low end of the cable run. The turnbuckle should be sized and rated for the cable size, the total span, and the maximum weight load of your zipline.

**Loop the cable** (use only braided, stainless-steel cable rated for zipline usage) through the eyebolt on the high side, place a metal thimble at the loop, and then secure it in place with three cable clamps.

**Thread the cable through an old tire** that will be positioned at the end of the run (on the downhill side) to work as a brake that prevents zipline riders from crashing into the tree or structure where the cable is secured. First, drill centered guide holes for the cable in opposite sides of an old, nonsteel-belted rubber tire. Also drill several ½" holes at the bottom of the tire tread to allow for water drainage.

**Secure the cable to the turnbuckle at the low end.** The turnbuckle should be loosened almost all the way so you can tighten the cable. Pull the cable through the turnbuckle as tightly as you can, and then lock it in place with three cable clamps. Test the tension in the cable, and tighten the turnbuckle, as needed.

**Clip the handle or trolley onto the cable** according to the manufacturer's instructions and test out the zipline, taking care to follow all safety precautions.

## LAUNCHING PADS

**If your yard doesn't have much natural slope** you'll have to create the slope to make your zipline work. You can do this by attaching the high end of the line to a tree or structure with a higher access point, such as a second-level deck. Or, you can build a launching platform on the tree for the high spot. A launching pad with ladder access is a fairly easy project to build and will create a safe entry point for zipline users. See page 121 for information on treehouse-type platforms.

# Classic Tree Swing

A rope hung from a large tree may be a simple swinging apparatus, but kids and even adults will find it completely irresistible. The rope may be hung with just a knot at the bottom for gripping or it may support a swing seat or an old tire.

All that is really required to build a rope swing is a healthy tree, a length of heavy rope, and the ability to tie a good knot. Use ½-inch diameter or larger rope (larger is better) made of nylon or hemp. Tie a few knots in the bottom of the rope as grips and to prevent unraveling, even if you plan to add a swing seat. Watch the rope for signs of wear, and test it often. Make sure smaller children understand how to use it safely, and that they should never make loops in it.

When siting your swing, look for a tree that has a sturdy limb at least 8 inches in diameter and nearly horizontal. The limb should be at least 10 feet above ground, and the swinging area should be free and clear of all obstacles, including the tree trunk, which should be at least 6 feet from the point where the swing is tied (further if the rope is longer than 10 feet). Landing and access areas should be clear of hazards and have shock-absorbing mulch or ground cover. Do not allow small children to use the swing without adult supervision.

## TOOLS & MATERIALS

½"-dia. rope or larger (nylon or hemp)

⅝"-dia. hot-dipped galvanized eyebolt with washer and nut

Metal thimble (to match rope)

Old tire (optional) or swing

Drill and spade bit for eye bolt

Stepladder

Eye and ear protection

Work gloves

**A tree swing** can be installed practically anywhere that you have a tree, clear swinging area, and safe spots for landing and access.

# How to Hang a Tree Swing

**Attach a ⅝" galvanized eyebolt** through the center of a branch that's at least 8" in diameter. Insert a thimble through the eye bolt; then tie the rope onto the eyebolt, threading it through the thimble to make the top curve. This is a tree-friendly approach to hanging a swing

**OPTION:** Tie the rope to the tree. If the branch is too high to easily reach with a ladder, throw a small cord with a weight over the branch, then use it to pull the rope up. Tie a loop in the end of the rope and pull it tight. Test the knot to make sure it is secure and does not slip.

**NOTE:** Wrapping a rope or chain around a tree limb is okay as a short-term swinging solution, but it can actually cause more long-term harm to the tree than an eyebolt. Prolonged friction from a tight rope can eventually start to strangle the limb by cutting through the bark.

##  ROPE SELECTION

**Use ½"-dia. or larger nylon or hemp rope** for a rope swing. Hemp is a traditional rope for swings, but will eventually start to rot if left out year-round. Nylon is almost indestructible, but will stretch slightly and is more expensive than hemp. Nylon is available in fun colors. A 12" galvanized steel eyebolt with thimble inserted into the eye offers a safe, tree-friendly hanging method.

**Hang the tire or swing seat.** Swings are an excellent use for an old tire, but avoid steel-belted types with exposed steel strands and clean the tire thoroughly before using it. Drill large holes in the tread of the tire to drain water away (inset). Do not use hard objects or objects with sharp corners (such as wood planks) as tree swings—they can cause damage or injury.

# Jungle Gym

The first known jungle gym—a framework of bamboo cubes—was developed by a mathematician as a way of teaching his children about three-dimensional space. It never caught on as a teaching aid but eventually became quite popular on playgrounds and has since become the progenitor for a wide variety of climbing structures.

Although earlier mass-marketed playground versions of jungle gyms were made from welded metal, most jungle gyms for home use today are constructed of wood or a combination of wood and metal. Because playground falls are not uncommon, it's recommended that you line the area beneath the jungle gym with a thick layer of mulch (see page 15). Sand any rough, splintery areas and round over all sharp edges before you assemble the jungle gym.

This jungle gym is made from scratch using pressure-treated lumber held together with lag bolts. Because the chemicals used to treat lumber these days are very corrosive, be sure to use triple-dipped zinc plated or stainless-steel bolts, washers, and nuts.

The climbing rungs (monkey bars) on this jungle gym are made from 1 inch inside-diameter galvanized water pipe. If you'd rather not cut all that pipe, you can buy prefabricated monkey bars at just about any larger building center and online. The assembly process we used is fairly straightforward: you simply create the six wood frames that make up the structure and then bolt them together, with the monkey-bar "ladder" connecting the two large side frames. Small children should use the jungle gym only under adult supervision.

## MATERIALS

| | |
|---|---|
| Lumber | (3) ⅜"-dia. × 33" |
| 2½" deck screws | threaded rod |
| Carriage bolts with | with nuts/washers |
| washers and nuts | |
| (⅜ × 2½", ⅜ × 4½", | Sandpaper |
| ⅜ × 5") | Eye and ear protection |
| 1¼" o.d. galvanized pipe | Work gloves |

**Climbing never gets old.** This jungle gym is simple to build but challenging enough to keep the kids busy for hours.

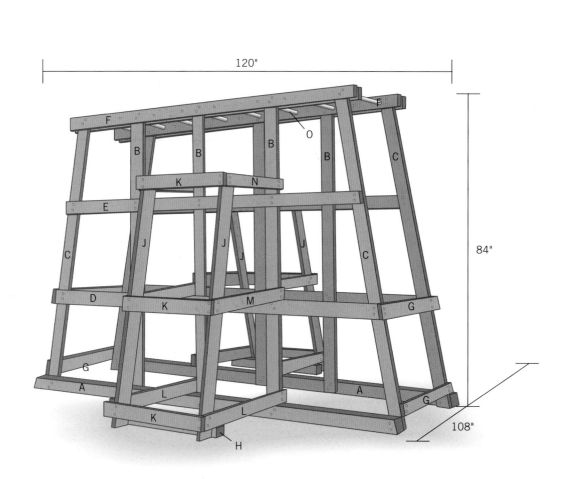

## CUTTING LIST

| KEY | NO. | DIMENSION |
|-----|-----|-----------|
| A | 2 | 3½ × 3½ × 120" |
| B | 6 | 1½ × 3½ × 84" |
| C | 4 | 1½ × 3½ × 86" |
| D | 2 | 1½ × 3½ × 111¾" |
| E | 2 | 1½ × 3½ × 100½" |
| F | 4 | 1½ × 3½ × 96" |
| G | 4 | 1½ × 3½ × 36" |
| H | 2 | 3½ × 3½ × 33" |

| KEY | NO. | DIMENSION |
|-----|-----|-----------|
| J | 4 | 1½ × 3½ × 61½" |
| K | 6 | 1½ × 3½ × 30" |
| L | 4 | 1½ × 3½ × 37½" |
| M | 2 | 1½ × 3½ × 32¼" |
| N | 2 | 1½ × 3½ × 26¼" |
| O | 7 | 1¼ o.d. × 29" galv. water pipe |

*All lumber is exterior-rated.

# How to Build a Jungle Gym

**1**

**Assemble the frames.** The jungle gym structure is composed of six frames that are built individually and then squared and bolted together. Start with the large side frames, laying out the rails and uprights so the distances between rails are equal. Tack each joint with a single 2½" deck screw.

**2**

Large side frame

**Start by cutting all of the rails and uprights** for the six frames to length. The ends of the outer uprights and the intermediate rails are cut at a 12° angle. After cutting and before assembly, thoroughly sand all of the parts to eliminate any slivers, rounding over any sharp edges as you sand.

**3**

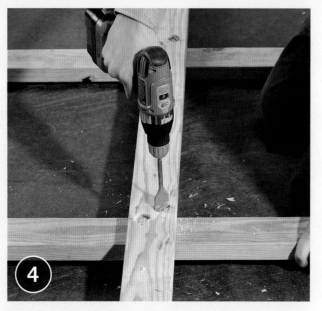

**4**

**Lay out the carriage bolt locations** once the frames are tacked together and squared. Use two bolts per joint. We used several lengths of ⅜"-dia., triple-dipped carriage bolts with the heads oriented on the outside faces of the frames. Joints where two 2 × 4s are assembled face-to-face require 2½" bolts; joints where a 2 × 4 is laid flat against the edge of another 2 × 4 require 4½" bolts. Mark the holes on the nut side of the joint.

**Drill counterbores for the washers** at the drilling points marked on the nut side of each joint. Mark a ½" drilling depth for each counterbore hole. Once the counterbores are all drilled, drill ⅜"-dia. guide holes through the counterbore centers using a spade bit. Drill all the way through the workpieces.

*(continued)*

**Insert a carriage bolt through each guide hole,** thread on a washer, and attach a nut. Attach all nuts in each frame, tightening by hand only. Once the entire structure is assembled and squared, then you should go in and tighten all nuts fully. Join the frames with carriage bolts driven through counterbored guide holes. The uprights in the large side frames are attached to 4 × 4 skids—use ⅜ × 5" triple-dipped bolts.

**Build and attach the wing assemblies** to the side frames as shown in the diagram. These assemblies are good for climbing, but they provide an even more important function in stabilizing the jungle gym structure.

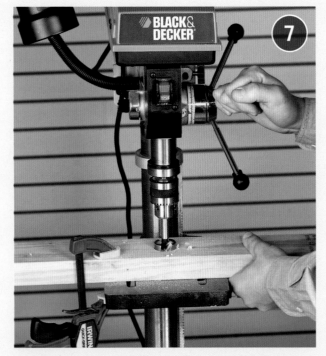

**Drill set holes for the monkey bars.** Mark drilling centers for the monkey bars on the inside faces of two 2 × 4 upper rails. The holes should be spaced 12" apart on-center. Mount a 1¼" Forstner bit in your drill press and set the drilling depth to 1". Drill the holes for the monkey bars. If you do not have access to a drill press, you can use a hand drill with a 1¼" spade bit.

**Cut the monkey bars to length** from 1¼" outside diameter galvanized water pipe. The best and safest tool for this is a metal cutoff saw, but you can also use a metal-cutting blade mounted in a reciprocating saw. Be sure to secure the pipe before cutting.

**Install the monkey bars** in the upper-rail guide holes and clamp the rails together with bar or pipe clamps. Fit the assembly between the side frames and clamp the parts together. Attach the rails to the outer rails with carriage bolts installed through both rails and the uprights between the rails. Use ⅜ × 4½" carriage bolts.

**Cut and install 2 × 4 filler strips** to fit between the top ends of the uprights, sandwiched between the horizontal frame tops. The main purpose of these fillers is to eliminate pinching hazards where small hands can fit.

**Install 33"-long pieces of threaded rod** at each end and in the middle to draw the "ladder" sides together. Drill guide holes for the all-thread so they fit inside rungs and fasten with nuts and washers set into counterbores. Tighten the nuts evenly so the "ladder" doesn't rack. Do not overtighten.

**Add the ladder steps** between the side frames to create access to the monkey bars. Once all the parts are installed and the structure fits together squarely, use a cordless impact driver or a ratchet wrench to fully tighten all of the nuts onto the carriage bolts.

# Obstacle Course

Obstacle courses are the perfect way for kids of all ages to hone their physical abilities, from balance and agility to fine-motor movements. Not only will a simple obstacle course provide good challenges for your kids and their friends, but it will also provide hours of fun and will improve the abilities kids need for other sports. The entire obstacle course should be positioned on a base of soft wood mulch or shredded rubber.

**You can find an obstacle course** for just about any creature in any situation—from dogs to football players, soldiers to horses. A good obstacle course teaches as much as it tests. When it's built in a backyard for use by kids, it has to be fun.

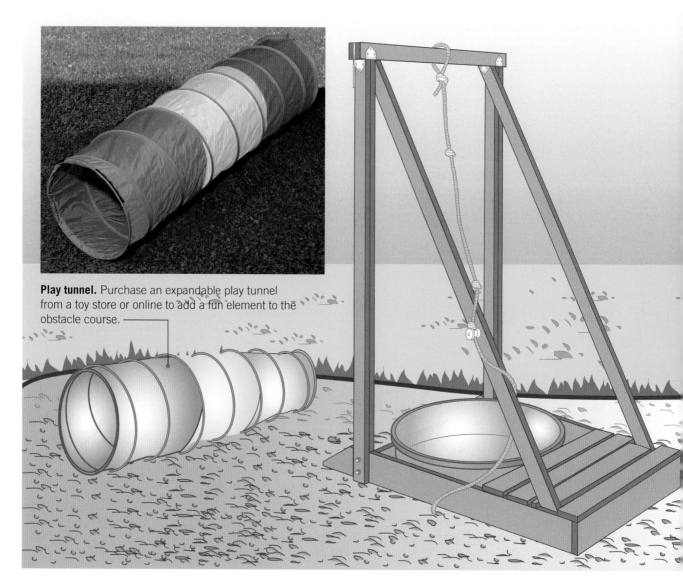

**Play tunnel.** Purchase an expandable play tunnel from a toy store or online to add a fun element to the obstacle course.

**Tire run.** This classic football test of footwork involves tires tied together. This lighter-duty version substitutes inflatable pool rings lashed together with bungee cords. You can anchor them with stakes as well.

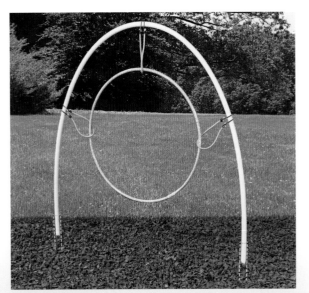

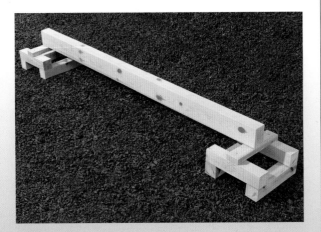

**Balance beam.** Make a central beam out of an 8' × 4" × 6" timber. Attach a 16 × 2 × 4" crosspiece to each end of the beam with 16d nails or deck screws. Set the beam on top of a stack of four 16 × 4 × 4" blocks to support the beam. Nail all the pieces together to keep them from shifting.

**Hoop jump.** Use a 10' length of ¾" PVC tubing and two 18" pieces of ½" CPVC tubing. Drive the CPVC stakes into the ground 40" apart, with 6" sticking up aboveground. Slip the open ends of the ¾" pipe over the stakes so that the pipe curves into an inverted U. Hang a standard hula hoop, centered, from the arch with bungee cords.

# Swinging Rope Challenge

This wonderful backyard addition can be added to the obstacle course on page 72 as yet another challenge for big and small kids alike, or it can be used as just a fun standalone feature in a backyard. In either case, its footprint is small, so it won't take up a lot of space, and the construction is all so straightforward that you won't spend more than a long Saturday building it. You can fill the pool with plain water, mud, or something really off the hook, like Jell-O. The idea is the same—grab the rope and swashbuckle across the pit to the other side. This is also an obvious candidate for summertime play as part of a water course that includes other super-fun features like a sprinkler jump and water slide.

**Grab the knotted rope** and swing across the pool of water for some jungle-inspired fun.

## TOOLS & MATERIALS

| | | |
|---|---|---|
| (4) 2 × 8" × 8' PT | Joist hanger nails | Construction adhesive |
| (7) 2 × 4" × 8' PT | Rope | Clamps |
| (2) 2 × 4" × 10' PT | Sand mats or mulch | Pencil |
| (2) 8' deck boards | 36 to 48"-dia. play wading pool | Tape measure |
| (8) ⅜ × 3" lag bolts with washers and nuts | Spool | Hammer |
| | Power saw | Eye and ear protection |
| Deck screws (3") | Drill/driver | Work gloves |
| (2) Post cap hardware | | |

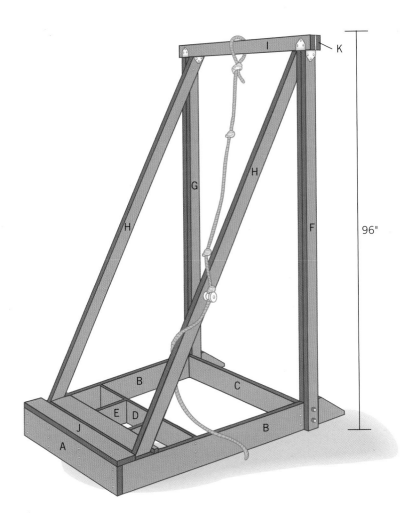

## CUTTING LIST

| KEY | PART | NO. | DIMENSION | MATERIAL |
|-----|------|-----|-----------|----------|
| A | Base end | 1 | 1½ × 7½ × 48" | 2 × 8 |
| B | Base side | 2 | 1½ × 7½ × 72" | 2 × 8 |
| C | Spacer | 1 | 1½ × 3½ × 45" | 2 × 4 |
| D | Deck rim | 1 | 1½ × 7½ × 45" | 2 × 8 |
| E | Deck joist | 4 | 1½ × 7½ × 21" | 2 × 8 |
| F | Outer post | 2 | 1½ × 3½ × 96" | 2 × 4 |
| G | Inner post | 2 | 1½ × 3½ × 88½" | 2 × 4 |
| H | Diagonal | 2 | 1½ × 3½ × 113" | 2 × 4 |
| I | Beam | 2 | 1½ × 3½ × 54" | 2 × 4 |
| J | Deck board | 4 | 5/4 × 5½ × 48" | Decking |
| K | Beam spacer | 1 | ¾ × 3½ × 54" | Plywood |

**Cut the base sides to length** and cut a 45° angle on one end of each side. Join the opposite ends of the sides by screwing them onto the ends of the end board with 3" deck screws. Screw the 2 × 4 spacer in place at the front, 5" in from the angled ends. Screw the deck joists to the inside of the end, spaced evenly across the end's span. Screw the inside ledger to the inside ends of the joists.

**Install the uprights.** Cut the inner and outer posts to length and attach them together with glue and 3" deck screws. Set each assembly onto the top edge of the base, 12" in from the front (profiled) end. Attach each post with a pair of counterbored ⅜ × 3" lag bolts.

**Mark and cut the diagonal braces.** Place a 10' 2 × 4 in position so one end fits into the back inside end of the base and the other crosses the top of each upright post. Mark cutting lines on the 2 × 4s, cut to length, and angle according to your cutting lines. Fasten the braces with lag bolts.

**Install the beam.** Attach adjustable post caps to the tops of the inner and outer posts and then fasten them to the uprights with joist hanger nails. Cut a beam to length from doubled 2 × 4s and set it onto the post cap saddles. Adjust the movable half of the cap and secure all parts. Insert a ½" plywood spacer between 2 × 4 beam halves and secure into a fixed post cap.

**5**

**6**

**Cut deck boards to length** and screw them down onto the deck joists. Make cutouts to fit around the diagonal braces if needed. There should be a gap of ¼" between deck boards.

**Tie the swinging rope securely to the top beam** and tie knots into the rope for grabbing points. Attach an empty thread spool or another object to the outside face of a diagonal brace to make a resting point for the rope so it can be reached from the deck.

## WATER SLIDES

If your kids would rather be found in the water than swinging over it, you can make your own water-park style water slide with only a roll of plastic sheeting and a hose. Buy a roll of 6-mil, 10'-wide (or larger) polyethylene sheeting. Roll it out and unfold it, preferably on a slope if you have one. Consider weighing down the edges with pieces of wood or other heavy objects so the plastic doesn't blow away (make sure wood is sanded smooth and finished to avoid splinters). Then, turn the hose on and spray water over the length of the plastic. The water will be cold at first, but it warms up quickly on the plastic. Add baby shampoo liberally, both on the plastic and on yourself; then take a running start and dive onto the plastic. Dish soap will also work, but baby shampoo doesn't sting if you get it in your eyes.

# Home Sports

There's no need to foot the bill for an expensive gym membership when you can turn your home's outside spaces into the perfect sporting arena. With just a little bit of effort, you can accommodate the entire family's sporting preferences, from the hoop dreams of your aspiring NBA star to your daughter's goal of being the next big skater phenom. It's just a matter of using the available space to its best advantage.

The beauty of adding a sports feature around the house is that it makes valuable exercise easy, convenient, and even fun. It's a way to add value and usability to spaces outside the house that might otherwise be nothing more than static landscape. Most of the projects in this section can be enjoyed by all members of the house, and can be a great way to bring the family together in wholesome activities.

The projects range from exceedingly easy to somewhat more challenging construction. But all can be built with basic tools and run-of-the-mill DIY skills. None will break the bank, but you should take care to always keep safety front of mind whenever you're building structures to accommodate sporting activities. The last thing you want is for injury to interrupt the fun.

## In this chapter:
- Skateboard Ramp
- Basketball Hoop
- Bocce Court
- Horseshoe Pit
- Tetherball
- Pickleball
- Putting Green
- Ladder Golf
- Beanbag Toss

# Skateboard Ramp

Because good places to practice can be few and far between, every skateboarder dreams of having a skateboard ramp of his or her own. Sidewalks may get dull, city streets are dangerous, and most public areas are rarely skateboarder-friendly; but your own ramp in your own yard is always ready and available.

This skateboard ramp (knowledgeable boarders would describe it as a mini half-pipe ramp) is a fun, challenging, and safe place to learn new skills—and it offers a softer landing than a hard concrete sidewalk. It's also fun to build and can be constructed in two to four days using only standard hand and power tools.

This 4-foot-high ramp measures 24 feet long by 8 feet wide. It is built in three sections: a pair of curved ramps on each end and a flat stretch in between. To keep the plywood that forms the curves from wicking up moisture and rotting, build it on top of concrete footings or pads. If you build it on a flat driveway or patio, set the corners and center transitions on concrete pads to keep the wood dry.

## TOOLS & MATERIALS

¾" exterior plywood

⅜" exterior plywood (sanded)

2 × 4 lumber (pressure-treated)

2 × 4 lumber (no. 2 or better)

Deck screws (1⅝", 2", 2½")

Lag screws (⅜ × 3") with washers

Carriage bolts (⅜ × 4") with washers and nuts

#6 panhead screws (1½")

Schedule 40 PVC tubing (2" dia.)

Jigsaw with wood-cutting blade

Power miter saw with stop blocks

Eye and ear protection

Work gloves

Skateboarding is a dangerous activity on ramps or anywhere else. Always wear a helmet, kneepads, and other protective clothing and equipment when skateboarding.

NOTE: This ramp is based on a free plan designed by Rick Dahlen and available for downloading. See Resources, page 141.

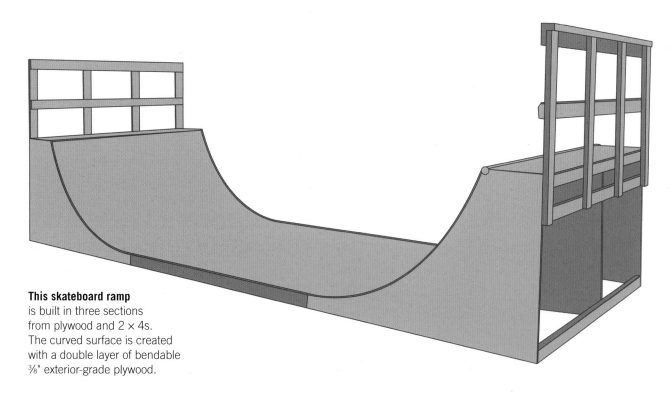

**This skateboard ramp** is built in three sections from plywood and 2 × 4s. The curved surface is created with a double layer of bendable ⅜" exterior-grade plywood.

# How to Build a Skateboard Ramp

Sleepers

**Mark the curves for the ramp sides** using a modified trammel. First, lay two sheets of ¾"-thick exterior plywood next to each other on a flat surface. The long edges should be touching, with the ends flush. Cut a thin strip of wood to 8' long and tack one end 3½" up from one of the back ends. Measure 7'6" from the point where the trammel strip is tacked and drill a ⅜"-dia. guide hole for a pencil. Insert a pencil into the guide hole and trace a curve on the plywood. Mark four pieces of plywood this way.

**Cut out the curves** using a jigsaw equipped with a fast wood-cutting blade. Watch the lines carefully as you cut to avoid drifting away from the curve, and make sure both the workpiece and the waste are well supported. Setting the plywood on 2 × 4 sleepers creates access space for the jigsaw blade.

**Cut notches for the coping pipe** at the top of each curved plywood upright, using a jigsaw. The notches allow the PVC coping pipe that is used to overhang the ramp slightly.

**Build the ramp side assemblies.** Cut the 2 × 4 spreaders to length using a power miter saw equipped with a stop block for uniform lengths. Install the spreaders between pairs of ramp sides at intervals of approximately 8". Drive several 2½" deck screws through the plywood and into the ends of the spreaders at each joint.

**Construct the 2 × 4 platform** for the flat middle area in two sections and then fasten the sections together with deck screws. Alternate driving directions between frames to create a stronger joint.

**Bevel the top spreaders.** Two spreaders are butted together at the top of each ramp to create a cradle for the coping tube (here, a piece of 2" PVC pipe). Butt a spreader up against the face of the top spreader in each ramp and mark a bevel cut on the edge so you can trim the spreader to be flush with the plywood base. Rip the bevel cut on a table saw or clamp the workpiece securely to a support board and cut the bevel with a straightedge guide and a circular saw. Set the saw blade angle to match the bevel angle.

**Join all the curved and flat sections with deck screws,** aligning the edges carefully. By this time, you should have moved the parts to the installation area and confirmed that the area is flat. Ideally, the ramp should be installed on a concrete slab or concrete footings that minimize ground contact.

Coping tube shown cutaway for clarity

**Add the coping tube** to the tops of the ramps—we used 2"-dia. Schedule 40 PVC tubing, but you can use rigid conduit or water pipe if you prefer metal. Drill eight evenly spaced ³⁄₁₆" holes through the coping, then enlarge the entry holes to ½". Fasten the coping to the beveled top spreaders with 1½", #6 panhead screws. *(continued)*

**Install a layer of ¾" plywood** to the flat areas of the ramp using 2" deck screws driven every 8" into the platform frames. Choose exterior-rated plywood with a sanded face facing upward to create a smooth skateboarding surface. Make sure joints between panels fall over 2 × 4 supports and make sure all screw heads are recessed slightly below the wood surface.

**Attach a double layer of ⅜" plywood** to the curved parts of the ramp. Standard ¾" plywood is too thick to bend along the ramp curves, so we used two layers of ⅜" plywood, which is limber enough to manage the gradual curves of the ramp. Make sure the seams for both layers are offset by at least 18" and that all joints fall over 2 × 4s. Leave ⅛" gaps between sheets for expansion and drainage. Attach with 1⅝" deck screws driven every 8".

**TIP:** To help the plywood bend more easily, dampen the reverse side.

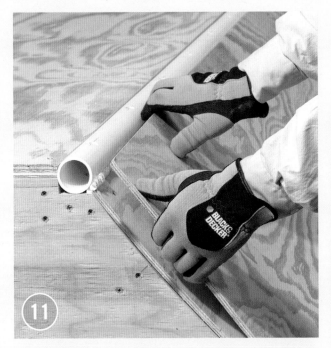

**At the joint between the coping and the deck,** spread a bead of caulk along the top edge of the first layer to keep water from wicking in between the sheets and rotting the wood. Caulk the gap between the coping tube and the first course before you butt the second course of plywood up to the coping. Fasten the plywood with 2" deck screws.

**TIP:** For a better joint, bevel-rip the top edge of the second course slightly.

**Bolt 2 × 4" × 4' posts to the back of each platform** using ⅜ × 4" carriage bolts. Attach an additional 2 × 4" × 4' corner post at each side to create L-shaped corners. Draw the corner post boards together with 2½" deck screws, closing the joint.

**Install horizontal rails** between the posts and then top-off each end rail system with a 2 × 4 cap plate attached with 2½" deck screws.

**Sand the plywood** to eliminate roughness and splinters, and set any protruding screws beneath the surface of the plywood. Vacuum the dust off, then coat all wood with paint or wood preservative. For best protection and ease of cleaning, coat the entire ramp with two or three thin coats of gloss exterior paint.

# Basketball Hoop

Basketball is one of the few sports where you can have as much fun competing against yourself as you can competing with others. If you have kids (or even if you don't), a basketball hoop in the driveway or backyard is an excellent investment.

A huge range of basketball hoops are available. Which one to select depends on your needs, your budget, and your yard or driveway. A hoop can be as simple as a metal rim screwed to the side of a garage or as elaborate as a heavy-duty, professional-quality system supported by a 48-inch-deep concrete base with 6-foot-wide tempered glass backboard (not to mention a professionally installed court with permanent markings). Within this range, the main choices are a portable goal (a pole and backboard supported by a wide, heavy base on wheels); a wall-mounted or roof-mounted backboard and goal; or

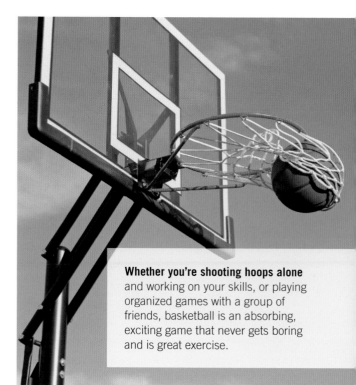

**Whether you're shooting hoops alone** and working on your skills, or playing organized games with a group of friends, basketball is an absorbing, exciting game that never gets boring and is great exercise.

a freestanding post set in concrete, with backboard and rim attached. You can buy any of these types with the basket and backboard fixed in place, or you can choose a goal that has an adjustable height feature—a good option if you have small children.

## Basketball Goals

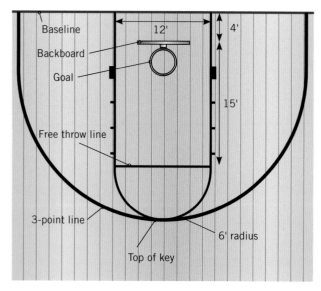

**Court Layout.** For a regulation half-court game (or full-court, if you have the space), tape off and paint your own home court or buy a stencil kit from a sports supply store.

**A backboard** is easy and fun to make from ¾" exterior grade plywood. Cut the shape with a jigsaw and seal all cut edges with wood preservative before priming and painting white. Use paint or tape to create the black outlines and the orange target box.

# Freestanding Goals

**A traditional basketball post is set in concrete.** This works well when you have a dedicated space for the court, as shown here.

# Wall-mounted Goals

**Wall-mounted goals** can be attached directly to the gable area of a garage or secured by angled support arms that are attached to a low-slope roof.

# Direct-mounted Goals

48"-deep footing

**Heavier backboards and posts** require a more substantial concrete base. The welded base plate is bolted to large J-bolts buried in the reinforced concrete base. Adjust the nuts underneath the plate to make the pole perfectly plumb. The concrete base is 48" deep (minimum) and 16" or more in diameter, with metal rebar inserted to help anchor the J-bolts. This type of post set-up is typically expensive.

**A glass goal** is bolted directly to support arms that are attached to the post. In many cases the goal can be lowered from the standard 10' height if you have smaller children.

# Bocce Court

Like many sports and games, bocce can be played casually on any reasonably level lawn with a minimum of rules, depending on how flexible you and your playing companions are. But if you are serious about playing bocce as a pastime and you have the space in your yard, consider building a regulation bocce court with a smooth, flat surface and a permanent border.

Developed in Italy as a variation of an ancient Roman game and then spread around the world, bocce is played at clubs, public courts, and backyards all over the world. Although not an Olympic sport, various bocce federations and clubs organize tournaments for enthusiastic amateurs, and competition can be fierce.

Official bocce courts for tournament play are 13 feet wide by 91 feet long, but recreational courts can be anywhere from 8 to 14 feet wide and 60 to 91 feet long. If you're trying to squeeze a court into your backyard, you can adjust those measurements as needed. Often the game is played without a court at all, or with an irregular-shaped court that

**Bocce is a popular backyard game** that has been around for centuries. It can be played free-form in any backyard, but for the truly authentic bocce experience you'll want a hard-surface bocce court.

accommodates the dimensions and shape of your yard. Standard courts are made from gravel topped with a fine clay or shell mixture and surrounded by a low wood wall, with the depth and composition of gravel and the construction of the wood wall determined by local climate and soil conditions.

Borders should be made of wood, and can be constructed of 4 × 4s, 4 × 6s, 2 × 10s, or other combinations of sizes. No matter which size you use, the border should be protected from frost heave and moisture, either by anchoring it to 4 × 6 posts set in concrete below the frost line or by building it on a thick bed of gravel.

Large, pressure-treated timbers like 6 × 6s and 6 × 8s make an excellent border, but these can be difficult to work with unless you're using a bobcat. You can substitute built-up layers of 2× lumber and 4 × 4s instead, overlapping seams and nailing and bolting them together. Bolt or screw them together from the outside, so that there are no visible fasteners on the inside of the court.

## TOOLS & MATERIALS

| | |
|---|---|
| 4 × 6 pressure-treated timbers | Circular saw |
| 2 × 10 pressure-treated timbers | Concrete mix |
| | Drill and spade bits |
| 1½ to 2"-dia. drainage rock | Laser level |
| Compactable gravel | Stakes |
| Tennis court clay, crushed oyster shells or similar blend | Mason's string |
| | Flat-nose spade |
| Lag bolts, washers, and nuts | Hammer |
| | Shovel |
| 2½" deck screws | Trowel |
| Posthole digger | Power tamper |
| Gravel compactor | Construction adhesive |
| | Eye and ear protection |
| | Work gloves |

6" min.

1-2" tennis clay or oyster shells

4-6" fine gravel

Drain tile

4-6" coarse gravel

Concrete

**Frame the court** with wood planks or timbers supported by frost footings or a thick gravel pad. Build the court surface from coarse gravel topped with finer, crushed limestone or similar stone, topped with crushed oyster shells, tennis clay or other similar material.

## HOW TO PLAY BOCCE

Bocce is played between two players or two teams of up to four players each. Eight large balls and one small ball called a "pallino" are used. The pallino is thrown out first. The object of the game is to get one of the large balls as close as possible to the pallino. Knocking the other team's balls away from the pallino is acceptable. For a much more in-depth version of the rules, along with playing strategies and penalties, visit www.boccestandardsassociation.org and the United States Bocce Federation at www.bocce.com.

Composite

Clay

Pallino

**Bocce is played with a set of eight bocce balls and one target ball.** Introductory sets made from composites can be purchased for less than $50. A traditional set of bocce balls made from clay and imported from Italy costs considerably more, but is a near-necessity if you develop a serious attachment to the game.

# How to Build a Bocce Court

**Find or create a level area in your yard** and stake out the corners of the bocce court. See previous page for discussion of court dimensions. Strip back the sod from the court area with a sod cutter or a flat-nose spade.

**Excavate the topsoil in the court area.** A regulation bocce court should be dug out a minimum of 10" so the proper subbase material can be put in. If your plans are more casual, you can cheat this step a little as long as the ground in your yard is not soft enough that the court will sink.

**Dig postholes.** To support the walls (and prevent them from moving) set pressure-treated 4 × 6 landscape timbers every 4' around the perimeter of the court. Ideally, the timbers (installed vertically) should extend past the frostline for your area. The tops will be trimmed to about 6" above grade after they're set.

**Set the 4 × 6 timbers into the post holes,** with a 4 to 6" layer of drainage gravel at the bottom. Fill around the timbers with concrete, sloping the tops to shed water. After all of the posts are set and the concrete is dry, use a laser level to mark level cutting lines on all the post tops and then trim them to height with a circular saw or reciprocating saw.

**OPTION:** After cutting the posts to height, use a circular saw set at 45°, a planer, or a trim router with a chamfer bit to cut chamfer profiles into the tops of the posts. Cut the outer edge and side edges of each post. Do not cut a chamfer on the side that will butt against the court walls.

**Spread a 4 to 6" layer of drainage rock,** such as 1½" river rock, onto the court. Cover this with a 4 to 6" layer of compactable gravel and tamp the gravel thoroughly with a power tamper. Add more gravel and tamp until you have attained a very firm base that is at or slightly below ground level.

**Build the walls.** Lay pressure-treated 2 × 10 lumber around the perimeter inside the posts. This first layer of the wall should be laid on edge, with the end seams falling at post locations. Fasten the boards to the posts with counterbored lag bolts, washers, and nuts. Then, attach a second layer of 2 × 10 inside the first layer. Use heavy duty construction adhesive and 2½" deck screws driven through the outer layer and into the inner layer.

**Add a 1"- to 2"-thick top layer of court clay,** crushed oyster shells, or other suitable medium. Here, crushed stone is being raked in preparation for compaction. Some top-dress layers do not require tamping, as the material will settle naturally. If the surface remains loose, however, you can use a power compactor to harden the surface so the bocce balls will roll more easily.

# Horseshoe Pit

### RULES FOR HORSESHOES

Stand by the stake at one end of the court and throw the horseshoe to the other end. If your horseshoe rings the stake (a ringer), you get three points. If no one gets a ringer, you get one point if your horseshoe is right next to the stake. Each player gets two horseshoes, and the first player to get 21 points wins.

Horseshoes and a similar game called quoits—which is played with rings instead of horseshoes—both evolved out of games played by soldiers in ancient Greece and Rome. In the United States, horseshoes was popular in both the Revolutionary and Civil War. Returning soldiers brought it back with them to their towns and farms, where it quickly took root, largely because most households already had all the equipment needed to play it—a few unattached horseshoes and two metal stakes.

According to the National Horseshoe Pitchers Association, regulation court size is 48 feet from end to end, with 40 feet in between goal stakes. Stakes are made of 1-inch-diameter steel 36 inches in length, and angle toward one another at 12 degrees. From 14 to 15 inches of post should protrude above ground. Horseshoes must not weigh more than 3 pounds. The ideal surface for the "pit" that cushions the horseshoes when they land and stops them from kicking up clods of dirt is moist blue clay, but sand or even loose dirt are acceptable.

Horseshoes are pitched from behind a foul line 37 feet away from the opposite stake, but the official rules allow women, children under 18, and men over 70 to pitch their horseshoes from 27 feet away from the opposite stake, if they so desire.

**Horseshoes has been played for thousands of years,** and is an easy game to set up in the back or side yard. A permanent horseshoe pit is a fun, easy project to build.

# Creating a Horseshoe Pit

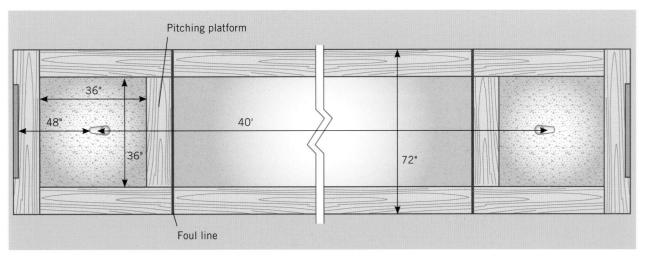

Pitching platform

36"

48"

40'

72"

36"

Foul line

**A typical horseshoes court.** The most important dimension to know for horseshoes is that you need 40' between the stakes. Other lines can be added with lime or other sport field marker as you become more serious about the game.

**A regulation horseshoe pit is a 3' square with 4" of loose sand on top.** The stake is a 1" steel rod or pipe sticking 14" out of the ground and angled away from the backstop at 12°. The backstops (optional but a very good idea) are made from pressure-treated 2 × 8 lumber attached to 2 × 4 stakes driven into the ground. They are 4' from the stake. Inset: An integral backstop and side arms form a cozy pit that keeps horseshoes under control, even if it doesn't quite meet the official regulations.

# Tetherball

A favorite at summer camps, tetherball is a simple but vigorous game for two people that involves hitting a ball on a rope back and forth around a pole until one player manages to wrap the ball completely around the pole. There is no governing body and little in the way of formal competition, but a basic set of rules has evolved to make the game fair and competitive, because otherwise a server who knows how to hit the ball will win every time.

Kits with metal poles and balls are available, but you can save money and get a sturdier pole if you make your own from galvanized pipe and then buy the ball with attached rope separately. The pole must be long enough to extend 10 feet above ground level, and the ball should hang 2 feet above the ground. To make a strong, removable pole, set a 2-foot length of pipe with a threaded coupling in a concrete base; then thread the 10-foot pole with an eyebolt at the top into the coupling.

Tetherballs with rope attached are available at sporting goods stores and on the Internet. Unless you're an experienced player, buy the soft version of the ball—it's easier on kids' hands.

## TETHERBALL RULES

Number of players: Two

The serve: Players stand on opposite sides of a 20'-diameter circle. The server begins play by hitting the ball around the pole in one direction. The opponent hits the ball around the pole in the other direction. The first player to wrap the rope completely around the pole is the winner.

Fouls: If a player commits a foul (see below), play stops and the player making the foul must give up his turn.

1. Hitting the ball twice at the serve before the opponent hits the ball

2. Hitting the tetherball with a part of the body other than one's hand or forearm

3. Holding, catching, or throwing the ball while play is ongoing

4. Stepping over the centerline

5. Reaching around the pole to hit the ball

6. Hitting the ball twice on your side of the court

7. Touching the pole

8. Hitting or touching the rope

**Tetherball** is a fast-moving game with plenty of hitting and jumping that fits easily into a small backyard.

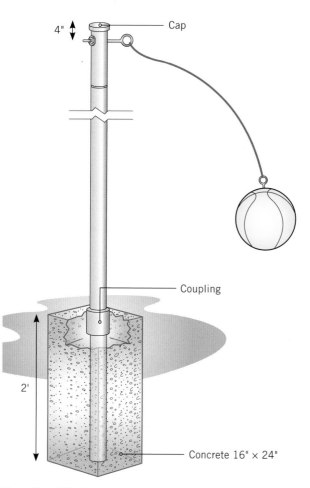

Cap

4"

Coupling

2'

Concrete 16" × 24"

**Dig a 2' × 16" hole,** set the assembled pole in the center, and plumb it in both directions with wood braces. Fill the hole with concrete to just below the top of the coupling, then slope the concrete to the outside so water doesn't pool around the pipe. Use plenty of pipe thread compound when you assemble the sections of pipe to protect the threads from rust and make it easier to remove the pole if it becomes necessary. Tighten the pipe with a pipe wrench so it doesn't loosen during play.

# Pickleball

Pickleball is a relative newcomer to the world of backyard games. With elements of tennis, badminton, and ping pong, it is played on a court roughly half the size of a tennis court (identical to a doubles badminton court) using paddles and a lightweight plastic ball. Despite the name, pickles are neither used nor consumed during play—the game was named in honor of the family dog of one of the co-inventors of the sport.

The pickleball court is 20 feet wide—the same width as a two-car driveway—and can be played on asphalt, concrete, wood, clay, or plastic-tiled sports courts. The USA Pickleball Association organizes tournaments and sells an official rulebook, though the basic game is simple to learn (see Resources, page 141).

**Pickleball is played with wood or graphite paddles,** hollow plastic balls, and a net (a badminton net will work).

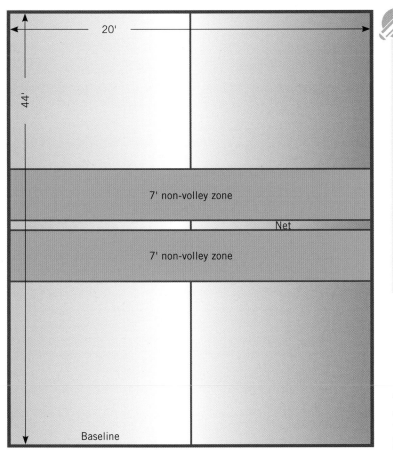

20'

44'

7' non-volley zone

Net

7' non-volley zone

Baseline

## PICKLEBALL RULES

The game starts with a serve (always underhand) from the right court to the right court on the other side, like tennis. On the first serve the ball must bounce once before the opposing team can return it, then bounce once before the serving team hits it back. After those two bounces it can be returned in the air or after bouncing once. You can only score when serving, and you score when the other team has a fault, such as missing the ball, hitting it into the net, or knocking it out of bounds. If the serving team faults, the other team serves. The first team to reach 11 with a 2-point margin wins.

**The official pickleball court size** is 20' wide and 44' long, with a 7' non-volley zone by the net. The net is 36" high at the sides and 34" high in the center.

# Putting Green

Serious golfers often say they "drive for show and putt for dough," and most of them practice putting at every opportunity. For these folks, a backyard putting green is the very definition of luxury.

Natural grass putting greens offer the ultimate in luxurious golf environments at home, but they require special breeds of grass and very specialized maintenance that very few people have the time or equipment to provide. But if you are willing to forego the smell of the fresh-cut Bermuda grass and the feel of a well-tended green underfoot, you'll find that there are a number of artificial putting green options that offer a chance to hone your putting stroke.

The panels and turf we used for making a putting green can be purchased on the Internet. The systems are easy to install and produce a good practice surface—a fine combination when it comes to putting greens.

## TOOLS & MATERIALS

| | | | | |
|---|---|---|---|---|
| Line trimmer | Utility knife | Turf spikes | Landscape fabric | Eye and ear protection |
| Heavy scissors | Hammer | Turf tape | Fabric staples | Work gloves |
| Screwdriver | Graph paper | Garden hose or rope | Chalk | |
| Jigsaw | Putting green panels | Spray paint | Straightedge | |
| Spade | Artificial turf | Sand | Rake | |

**Backyard putting greens** give golfers a whole new way to have fun and perfect their game. Special kits, including panels and artificial turf, make building one an easy weekend project.

# Designing a Backyard Putting Green

**Choose an above-ground green** for seasonal use or even to use indoors. They lack a bit of authenticity, but they are very convenient.

**Kit accessories,** such as pins and edge liners, give a backyard putting green a more genuine flavor. A chipping mat can be positioned around the green to let you work on your close-in short game without destroying your yard.

**Artificial turf** comes in an array of styles and lengths. Lower nap products, like the two samples to the left, are best for putting greens.

# How to Install a Backyard Putting Green

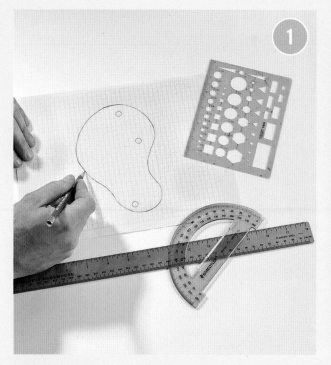

**Diagram your putting green on graph paper,** including cup locations. If you are ordering your kit from an Internet seller, they probably have a mapping and planning program on their website. Order panels and turf as necessary to create your putting green.

**As soon as it arrives,** unroll the turf and spray it with water to saturate. Set the turf aside and let it dry for at least 24 hours. This process preshrinks the turf.

**Measure the installation area** and mark the perimeter of the putting green, using a garden hose or rope. Lift the hose or rope and spray-paint the green's outline onto the grass. Some putting green kits are precut to create specific shapes and sizes, while others offer a bit more design flexibility.

**Inside the outlined area,** use a line trimmer to scalp the grass down to the dirt. Rake up and remove any debris.

**Add sand or remove dirt as necessary** to create contours in the putting green. Kit manufacturers suggest that you create the contours that replicate the breaks you most want to practice. For example, if you have trouble hitting uphill and to the right, create a hill and place the cup at the top and to the right.

**Cover the scalped and contoured installation area** with landscape fabric, overlapping seams by at least 2". Trim the fabric to fit inside the outline and secure it to the ground with landscape fabric staples.

**Starting in the center of the installation area,** push two panels together and hold them tightly in place as you insert the fasteners. Use a screwdriver to tighten the fasteners. Install the panels in locations indicated on your diagram.

**Continue to fill in panels,** according to your plan. Take special notice of putting cup locations. In many kits, these require special panels with cups preinstalled. Locate them according to your plan. *(continued)*

**Where panels go beyond the outline,** use a light-colored crayon or chalk to mark a cutting line. Avoid cutting into the interlocking panel edges.

**One panel at a time,** cut panels to shape, using a jigsaw with a blade that's slightly longer than the panel thickness. Use panel scraps to fill in open areas in the layout wherever you can, and then mark and cut the scraps to fit.

**Dig a 4"-wide by 4"-deep trench** around the perimeter of the green shape, directly next to the edge of the panels.

**Place the artificial turf on top of the panels.** Pay attention to the nap of the turf to make sure it all runs in the same direction. Use a utility knife to cut it to size, 4" larger than the panel assembly.

**Install the cups into the panels** containing the cup bodies, and then cut holes in the turf with a utility knife.

**Fold back the edges of the turf.** Apply double-sided carpet tape to the perimeter of the panel assembly. Peel off the tape's protective cover, then press the turf down onto the tape. Fold the excess turf over the edge of the panel assembly and down into the trench. If the turf bulges around a tight radius, make 3½" slashes in the edge of the turf and ease it around the curve.

**Drive carpet spikes or fabric spikes** (provided by the kit manufacturer) through the edges of the turf and into the trench to secure the turf.

**Backfill the trench with the soil you removed earlier.** Add landscaping around the edges of the green, if desired. Sweep and hose down the green periodically and as needed.

# Ladder Golf

**TOOLS & MATERIALS**

(3) ¾" × 10' CPVC
(6) ¾" CPVC T-fittings
(6) ¾" CPVC elbows
PVC primer and cement
⅜"-dia. × 20' nylon rope
(12) Solid-core golf balls
Hand screw (wood clamp)
Tubing cutter
Drill press and ⅜" bit
Sand
Electrical tape
Eye and ear protection
Work gloves

Ladder golf doesn't have much to do with golf, but it's plenty of fun and it's exploding in popularity. Stop by any tailgate party outside the football stadium and there's a good chance you'll see several fans engaged in a heated game. Also called ladder toss, ladder ball, and many other names (some not especially polite), ladder golf is a relatively new backyard game that involves tossing short bolas made from golf balls at a ladderlike stand. If the bola wraps around one of the ladder rungs and stays, you earn points. You can make your own ladder golf game in a few hours using PVC tubing, some ⅜-inch nylon rope, and a dozen golf balls in two different colors. It's best to make a pair of goals so all the players don't have to traipse back and forth after every turn, but a single goal is adequate to play.

**Ladder golf is a fun** (some would say addictive) backyard game that anyone can play. The goals and the golf ball bolas are easy and cheap to make yourself.

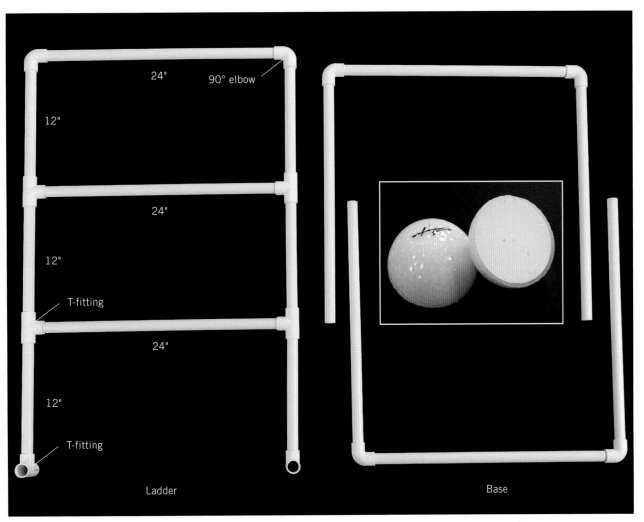

Labels in figure:
24" 90° elbow
12"
24"
12"
T-fitting
24"
12"
T-fitting
Ladder

Base

**Ordinary PVC tubing** is used to make the goals for ladder golf. You'll need six 12" lengths and nine 24" lengths, along with six tee fittings, sand, and six elbow fittings. Inset: Look for solid-core golf balls. Top-Flite is one common brand name that has a solid core. Balls with liquid or gel cores will leak unpleasant chemicals if you drill through the middle.

## LADDER GOLF RULES

Ladder golf can be played by any number of players or teams, with each player using three bolas. The top rung of the ladder is worth 3 points, the middle is 2 points, and the bottom is 1 point. The official throwing line is 15' from the ladder, but children and the elderly may play closer. Each player throws all three of their bolas before the next player has a turn, and the player who has exactly 21 points at the end of a round of play wins.

**Players are allowed to:**

- Throw the bola in any way they wish, including bouncing.

- Knock other players' bolas off the ladder, thus taking away their points.

- Distract opponents with questions, loud remarks and rude noises.

**Players are not allowed to:**

- Touch or hit opposing players, even gently.

If a player goes over 21 points in a round, none of that player's points for that round count. A player who wraps all three bolas around the same step or around each of the three steps during one round of play earns 1 extra point.

If more than one player gets 21 points, the tying players continue playing rounds until one of them finishes 2 points ahead of the other.

# How to Make Ladder Golf Goals

**1**

Cut all of the parts for each goal to length from ¾" CPVC tubing. If you have one, use a tubing cutter for clean cut. You can use a hacksaw instead and deburr the cut ends with emery paper.

**2**

Test fit the parts to dry-assemble each goal. In most cases, the fit between tubing and fittings is tight enough that a simple friction fit with no glue will hold the parts together. This has the added benefit of letting you disassemble the goal easily.

## PERMANENT CONNECTIONS

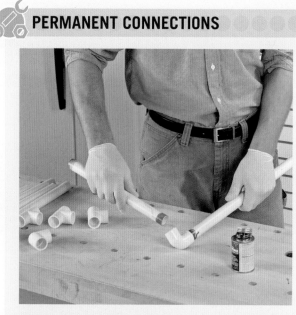

**Solvent-glue the parts together** for a permanent goal that will not fall apart during use. PVC primer alone will create a strong enough bond that the parts are unlikely to come apart, but if you foresee great stress, you can use solvent glue. One compromise option to gluing versus not gluing is to glue the parts of the upright together and to glue the parts of the feet together, but allow the joints where the uprights meet the feet to be friction-fit only. That way, the parts can be partially disassembled for easy storage and transport.

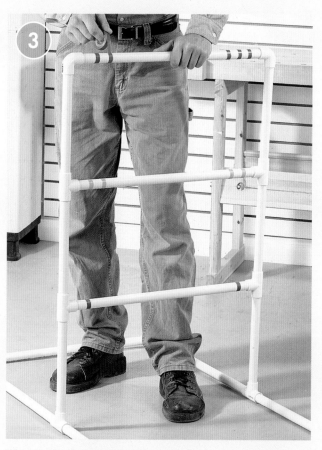

**3**

**Wrap bands of narrow electrical tape** (comes in multiple colors) around the scoring bars as a scoring reminder.

# How to Make Ladder Golf Bolas

**Secure a solid-core golf ball** (See page 103) into the jaws of a wooden handscrew clamp. It is very important that the ball be secured during drilling.

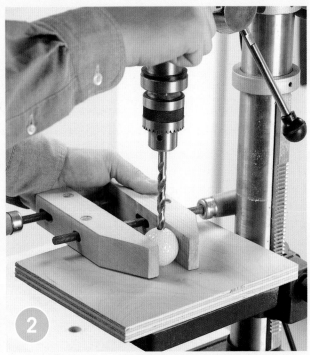

**Set the handscrew clamp with the golf ball** onto the table of a drill press and position it so the ball is centered under the point of a ⅜" bit. Drill all the way through the ball. You can use a drill without a drill press, but take great care and make sure the clamp is well secured to the worksurface.

**Feed ⅜" nylon rope through the hole** in a golf ball. Tie one end tightly to secure the golf ball, and then feed the other end through another golf ball. Tie that end so the distance between golf balls is 13".

**Trim the ends of the ropes** so about ½" sticks out from each knot. Carefully singe the nylon fibers so they melt together and will not unravel.

# Beanbag Toss

Beanbag toss was invented, by most accounts, during the darkness of the middle ages in Europe. Lost for centuries, it was rediscovered in the back woods of Kentucky in the nineteenth century. However, the basic idea of the game—throw something at a target—has existed uninterrupted for many thousands of years.

Little equipment is needed to play beanbag toss—just a pair of wooden boxes with holes and several small cloth bags filled with dried beans or corn. The object is to throw the beanbags into the holes. The two boxes are placed so that the holes are 33 feet apart for standard play, though you may move the targets closer for players with limited throwing range. Players stand to the side of a box when pitching. Each player gets four bags to throw. A bag that goes into the hole is worth 3 points, a bag that lands on the box and stays put is worth 1 point, and a bag that ends up off the box is worth nothing. The first player to 21 wins.

## MAKING BEANBAGS

You can purchase beanbags inexpensively at any toy store, or you can make your own using dry navy beans or unpopped popcorn and extra cloth. Make bags in sets of four, each from matching cloth. You'll need four bags per player. (Two to four players is typical). To make each bag, sew two 7" square pieces of duck cloth together on three sides, turn it inside out, and fill with two cups of dry beans or feed corn (it should be about 14 to 16 oz.). Tuck the open end into the bag, pin it and then sew it shut, and stitch around all the edges. The finished bag should be approximately 6 × 6".

**Despite its simplicity,** a serious game of beanbag toss can last for hours. Dried beans are the usual filler for the bags, though dried corn is preferred in some areas of the country.

# How to Make a Beanbag Toss Game

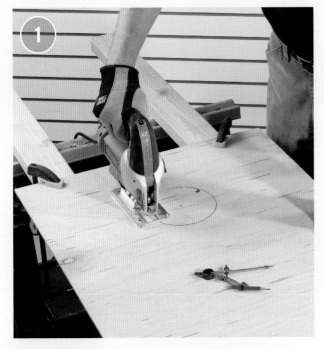

**Cut the plywood underlayment panel** into 24 × 48" boards using a circular saw and straightedge cutting guide (or a tablesaw if you have one). Lay out a 6"-dia. hole 6" down from the top of each panel and cut it out using a jigsaw.

**TIP:** Jigsaws cut on the upstroke, so cut from the underside of the panel (if it has one) to minimize tear out on the top. Sand the cut edges thoroughly to smooth the edges and remove splinters.

**Assemble the frame.** Drive 2½" decks screws at the corner joints, making sure the corners are square. Cut two 11½" long lengths of 2 × 4 for the legs for each target. Attach the legs by driving 2½" deck screws through the legs and into the inside of the target frame. Attach the top panel to the frame with panel adhesive and 4d finish nails.

**Prime and paint the target boxes.** Use exterior-grade paints. Add creative designs with acrylic hobby paints.. Select a fun pattern, such as the sunrays seen here.

# Special Section: Swimming Pools

A swimming pool can be many things in a backyard. It's a lovely water feature that adds immeasurably to the look of the yard and house. It's a refreshing luxury that allows you to cool off on even the hottest of summer days. It can be the centerpiece of outdoor parties from informal cookouts to wedding receptions. But more than any other role, the swimming pool is a fantastic place to de-stress and get regular exercise in one of the most pleasurable activities possible. Choosing the right pool for you and your family depends partly on budget and space available, but also on the particular uses for which you want to focus the pool.

**Entertainment.** Most pools for private home use are built and used for entertainment, whether alone, as a couple, as a family, or with friends, neighbors, and extended family.

**Relaxation.** Coupled with entertainment, there's the benefit of relaxation, of cooling off in the water on a hot summer day, or enjoying a soak in the evening.

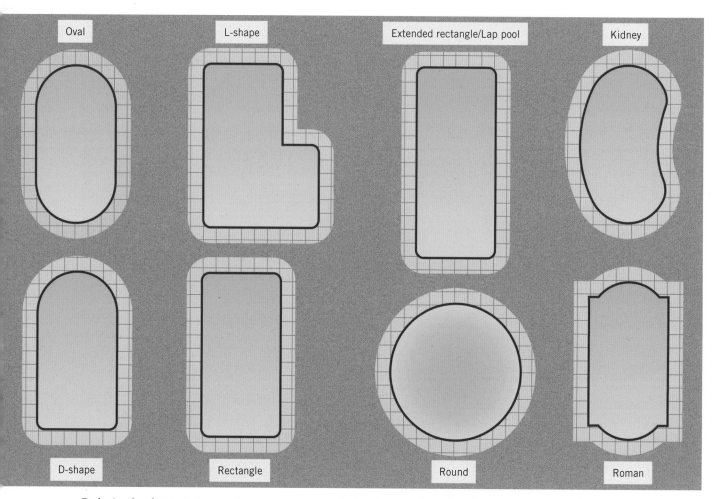

**Typical swimming pool shapes** give you several recognizable design options, but if you're using a vinyl liner or concrete pool walls and floor, the design possibilities are practically limitless.

**A custom-shaped pool** is an eye-catching feature in any yard and makes for interesting waterplay and poolside lounging.

**Housing value.** Homes with an in-ground pool add about 8 percent to the value of a residential property, according to a recent study by the National Association of Realtors; adding an in-ground pool to a $200,000 home, for instance, appreciates its value by $16,000 as soon as you fill it with water and fire up the pumps. (The same study found that above-ground pools add no discernible value to a home.)

**Exercise.** Swimming is one of the best low-impact aerobic exercises you can get.

**Design element.** Some pools are designed and built mostly as water features in the garden. Whether still or with movement facilitated by a pump and filter system, decorative pools bring the soothing and attractive element of water to the garden and become places to reflect alone or gather as a group.

# Concrete Pools

The traditional residential pool (if there is such a thing) is an in-ground pool with concrete walls and a concrete deck. While there are several advantages to going the concrete route, especially if you live in a temperate climate, more modern shell options have been taking over the home pool market in recent years.

The excavation for the concrete pool must be outfitted with reinforcement (typically metal rebar) to strengthen the concrete shell. When finished, the web of vertical and horizontal rebar resembles a metal cage in the same shape as the excavation, held about 4 inches out from the dirt sides and bottom of the pool. Other features, such as steps or integral seating, might be formed with plywood or rebar in preparation for concrete. In addition, a thicker "bond beam" along the top of the walls is formed with rebar to support the pool deck and coping.

Concurrently, the contractor will install (or "rough in") the pool recirculation system behind and within the rebar cage. This includes skimmer openings, the main drain, suction valves, and any automated cleaning, water feature, and/or lighting conduits that are to be run underground from the pool structure to the equipment set nearby. Once properly installed, the pipes, wires, and other conduits are located or "stubbed up" near the location of the equipment set, to be connected later; their openings in the pool

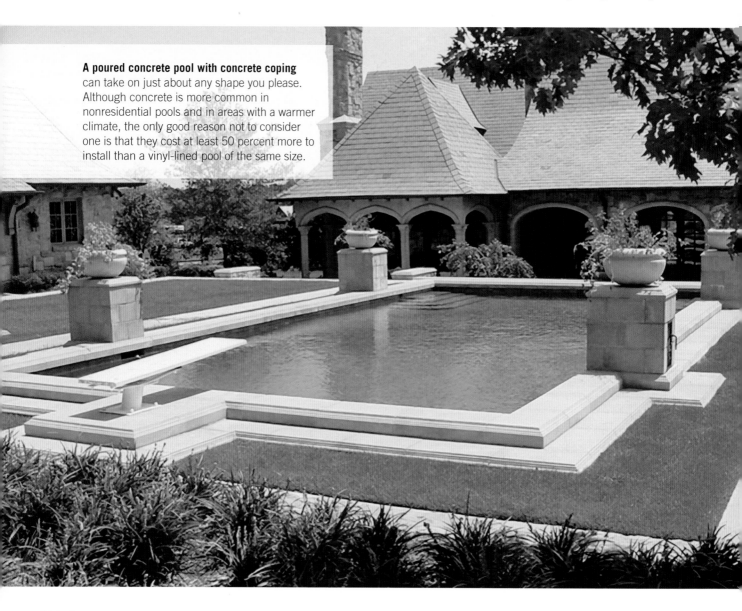

**A poured concrete pool with concrete coping** can take on just about any shape you please. Although concrete is more common in nonresidential pools and in areas with a warmer climate, the only good reason not to consider one is that they cost at least 50 percent more to install than a vinyl-lined pool of the same size.

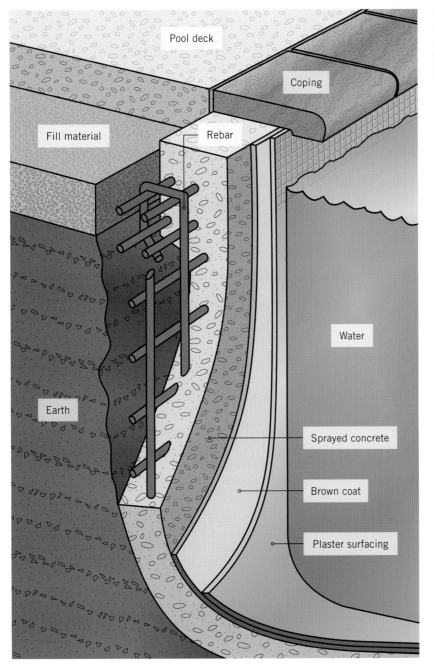

Pool deck

Coping

Fill material

Rebar

Earth

Water

Sprayed concrete

Brown coat

Plaster surfacing

**A concrete pool** is built much like a building foundation, with reinforced concrete walls and floor. Most concrete pools are coated with a surface layer of gunite or shotcrete.

shell are covered or otherwise protected during the construction process to keep dirt, construction debris, trash, pests, and concrete from clogging the system.

In recent years, pool builders have relied on one of two spray-applied methods (gunite and shotcrete) to create the shell of a concrete pool, all but replacing standard poured concrete and concrete masonry units in pool construction. These two spray-applied methods are more time-efficient and appropriate for concrete pool building. They are easier to control, faster to apply, adhere better to the excavated and reinforced sidewalls without significant sloughing (compared to traditional poured concrete methods), and enable the greatest amount of design flexibility.

After the pool walls are created, a cement-based finish is applied to the raw concrete surface. Ceramic tile is often added along the top several inches of the sidewalls as a decorative feature and as an easy-to-clean material at the waterline in plaster-finished pools.

Once the finish is cured (requiring perhaps another week), the pool builder or equipment installer finishes the systems rough-in with skimmer flaps, drain covers, outlet fittings, and, of course, the equipment set nearby. When the deck and any other landscape or integral water features and finishes are completed, the pool can be filled with water, cleaned and chemically balanced, and enjoyed.

# Vinyl-lined Pools

In-ground pools built using a vinyl liner are less expensive and faster to install than a concrete pool. Often called "packaged" pools, they are available in a limited—if increasing—variety of shapes and sizes, and are typically delivered with all the necessary components to complete the project.

Instead of reinforced concrete, an interlocking system of support members creates the structure of a vinyl-lined pool. These components, usually L-shaped, are engineered and made of aluminum, steel, plastic, or stainless steel; a contractor may also use concrete blocks or treated wood for below-grade projects. Regardless, these structural components create a solid shell for a thick, watertight vinyl membrane.

For in-ground, vinyl-lined pools, the excavation phase of the project is similar to that of a concrete pool, except that the hole must be dug large enough to accommodate the buttresses of the sidewall components, as well as the rough-in of the recirculation system and any accessory features serving the pool.

The pool bottom is leveled and covered (and leveled again) with sand, cement, or vermiculite to reduce the chance of tearing the liner. With the structure secure and level, the system's rough-ins in place, and the pool bottom ready, the liner is carefully unfolded and/or unrolled and gently pulled to the sides. The process is arduous, requiring several people and, especially toward the end, a good deal of strength. Folds, if any, are spread out or cut away.

With the liner securely in place and molded to any steps, seating, or other integral features (typically accommodated in the factory to maintain the liner's structural integrity), a contractor installs and connects the plumbing and lighting finishes and the equipment set, making the pool ready for water. Then the contractor fills in the excavated area behind the structural members with dirt (called backfill) to balance the pressure on both sides of the pool. The backfill also forms the base for the deck and coping material surrounding the pool.

The main concern about vinyl liners is their vulnerability to chemicals and UV rays, especially if the water chemistry is routinely unbalanced and unsanitary. Dry chlorine, for instance, must be completely dissolved in the pool water, perhaps mixed in a separate, non-metal bucket of water before being placed in the pool.

As with any pool, a regular schedule of careful and appropriate maintenance goes a long way to preserving the integrity and value of your investment. Care for it correctly, and a vinyl liner can last up to 15 years before it needs to be replaced from normal wear and tear.

**Vinyl pool liners** are taking over much of the residential pool market because they are the least expensive system and they offer low maintenance. Because the pressure from the weight of the water maintains the pool shape, in-ground vinyl pools cannot be drained.

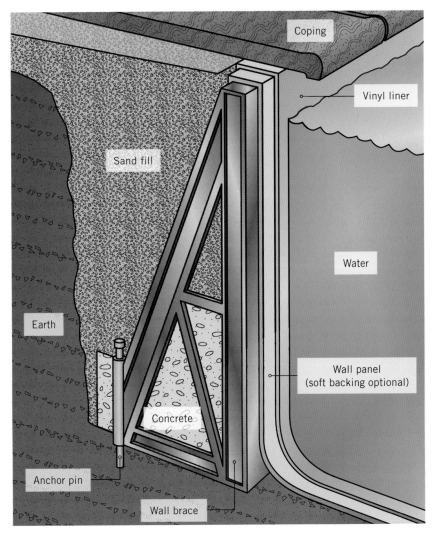

Coping

Vinyl liner

Sand fill

Water

Earth

Wall panel
(soft backing optional)

Concrete

Anchor pin

Wall brace

**In-ground pools with a vinyl liner** are low in maintenance, but the liners usually require replacement after 15 years or so. They may also develop leaks over time, which are normally repaired by a professional with the pool still full of water.

**Vinyl liners** are made in a dizzying array of colors and patterns that you may choose from when ordering your new pool or a replacement liner.

A swimming pool with a vinyl liner is a relatively fast pool type for professionals to install. The hole that is excavated for the pool has very low tolerance, however, so great pains are taken to get the shape leveled and finished. Any imperfections in the excavation will show through on the finished product.

Once the pool installation is complete, the pool deck is added. Often, the deck is made of poured concrete with integral coping that covers the tops of the pool support walls. Other materials, such as flagstone or concrete pavers, also may be used for the deck surface.

**The site is excavated to the sidewall depth,** then the walls are positioned and braced.

**The excavation is completed to final depth** at the deep end, usually with a backhoe.

**Plumbing and equipment are hooked up** and the shape of the excavation is refined. A concrete footing is poured around the perimeter of the pool wall.

**Soft wall panels are installed on the excavation walls** to provide cushion so the vinyl is less likely to tear. An additional cushion layer may be installed between the wall and the vinyl liner.

**The vinyl liner is placed into the pool excavation** and attached to the tops of the support walls. The area behind the walls is backfilled once all of the pool connections are made.

# Fiberglass Shell Pools

Fiberglass is a significantly less popular pool type than concrete or vinyl. In-ground fiberglass pools are very limited in their available sizes and shapes. This is mostly because, as factory-made shells, they must be built within certain dimensions to be safely transportable.

The excavation process for a fiberglass pool is similar to concrete and vinyl-lined projects; as with the latter, the contractor digs a hole a bit larger than the shell to accommodate the system rough-in components and to allow the installation crew to properly level the bottom and backfill against the outside of the pool walls.

Once the excavated area has been prepared and its bottom leveled or shaped to match that of the pool shell as closely as possible, the pool is hoisted from the delivery truck with a crane and carefully placed in the hole. Rarely will the first placement be perfect; more likely, the crew (using the crane) will have to lift the pool out and refine the excavation to ensure that the bottom of the pool is completely and reliably supported.

Eventually, the pool shell is unstrapped, steadied by temporary bracing, and connected to the recirculation system rough-in and above-ground equipment. The pool is filled with water and backfilled at the same time to balance the pressure on both sides of the walls. The backfill is typically wet sand that fills voids between the exterior shell walls and the excavated hole. To provide stability and drainage for the coping and deck material, some contractors lay a bed of crushed rock for the top 4 inches or so of the backfill.

In-ground fiberglass pools typically are more expensive than comparably sized and standard-shaped concrete pools. However, above-ground fiberglass pools are more cost-competitive, primarily because there is no excavation required. They are also smaller than other in-ground pools, requiring less water and fewer chemicals (and less expense) to maintain.

As with any pool, fiberglass is not immune to wear and tear. The inside gel-coat surface can become brittle and cracked from neglect and will wear out over time. Severe surface damage may even affect the fiberglass material behind the coating, requiring a patch that may necessitate re-excavation if it is serious enough to cause a leak. Fiberglass also cannot withstand a lot of weight on its edges; a pool deck or coping material, or stone edging that relies on the shell for structural support may buckle the fiberglass. As an alternative, fiberglass pool manufacturers are broadening the design options for the integral coping that's premolded into their products.

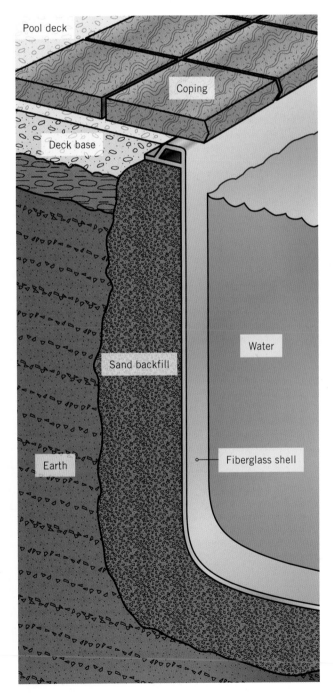

**Fiberglass pool shells** are simply set into the ground and wet sand is dumped in from above to backfill around the shell.

# Aboveground Pools

Long perceived as the cheap alternative to in-ground pools, the pools that stake their claim above ground have improved dramatically in appearance, durability, and performance in recent years.

Resins are now the rule for exterior shell materials, providing one-piece finishes that not only open up design options in color and pattern, but last longer than their predecessors. Inside shells (usually flexible liners), meanwhile, feature factory-applied patterns that replicate the tiled waterline borders of concrete pools, among other finishes. Manufacturers are also creating perimeter top edges that are 10 inches wide, providing enough surface area (and the perception of bulk) to meet demand from consumers who don't want or cannot accommodate a full deck around the pool.

Responding to smaller backyard lots in today's new housing landscape, aboveground pool makers have re-engineered the structural system to eliminate buttresses (the supports projecting from the exterior walls, as backfilling does for an in-ground pool), saving 6 feet or so in the overall width and length of the pool. Similarly, the latest above-ground pools are 50 inches or more deep to more closely resemble in-ground pool depths. Automation and better equipment have also crept into the market, and automatic cleaners and chlorinators are more common, along with more powerful pumps and filters.

To install an aboveground pool, you start by outlining and then leveling out the pool area to at least 4 feet beyond the pool footprint. Level the area

**Aboveground pools** may lack some of the cachet of an in-ground pool, but they are much more affordable and much more practical for many homeowners.

# INFLATABLE & TEMPORARY POOLS

The last distinct category of pool construction is inflatable and temporary pools. These aboveground products are truly mobile, though often as big (if not as deep) as any other type of pool, and requiring just a flat, clean surface and a garden hose. More sophisticated models feature attachable pumps and filters to circulate and help clean the water, as well as covers, cleaning accessories, and repair kits that make it easier to maintain them during heavy seasonal and multi-year use.

As their name implies, inflatable pools feature sidewalls filled with air to create a vessel for water. Some sport inflatable top collars that pull the sidewalls up to their full height as the pool fills with water. Similarly, temporary pools feature flexible sidewalls held up and in place by strategically spaced structural members and filled with water, and offer a consistent depth, usually about 4 feet.

Made with tough, thick vinyl (the thickest layer forming the bottom), inflatable and temporary pools can be up and ready to enjoy fast, and they tear down just as quickly. If they are to remain standing or filled for multiple uses or certainly a season, they can (and should) be sanitized and chemically balanced as a permanent pool to maintain their integrity and value.

Primarily, however, inflatable and soft-sided pools are an inexpensive and easy way to enjoy the water, and can be stored and moved simply, making them ideal for renters and budget-conscious homeowners. Such pools are also not considered "real" or taxable property, as a more permanent pool would be assessed, thus saving you a bit on your property taxes and homeowner insurance premiums.

**Inflatable and temporary pools** are being made in ever-larger sizes, dramatically increasing their appeal for backyard use. A recirculating pump with a small filter (inset) is the only equipment that accompanies most inflatable pools.

by removing high ground, taking care not to disturb the ground that remains behind. Then, you assemble a framework made from base rail plates that support uprights. A layer of sand is laid on the entire area, to create a smooth bottom and protect the pool bottom from rocks and sharp objects in the ground.

Once the framework, including the upright panels, is in place and the sand bed is laid, the liner fabric is draped over the frame, then held in place with plastic edging. Then, the top plates, rails, and cover are installed according to the pool instructions. The pumps and skimmer are attached as the pool is being filled. Typically, you'll need to make cutouts in the liner for the hookups. Make cutouts in the liner and install the skimmer and pump when the pool is a third full.

# Pool Safety

The importance of safety in and around your pool cannot be overstated. Simply, it is your primary responsibility as a pool owner to ensure the safety of everyone who enjoys it, cleans it, keeps the water balanced, or even just peers at it enviously over your privacy fence or self-latching gate.

Comprehensive pool safety encompasses several practical measures. Ideally, your pool was designed and built with safety in mind, including features such as a slip-resistant deck and coping, a secure perimeter fence and gate(s), the proper depth and dimensions for a variety of activities, and provisions for a safety-rated cover.

Other protections recommended by the U.S. Consumer Product Safety Commission (CPSC) to maintain a safe and healthy private swimming pool include: having lifesaving and first-aid gear close at hand, properly anchoring handrails and other accessory and accessibility features, and posting easy-to-read signs. A pool safety plan may also include lighting schemes, thermometers (to ensure safe water temperature), and a variety of alarms.

Safety also extends to how and where you store and use the chemicals needed to maintain a healthy water chemistry, as well as setting and enforcing rules of conduct in and around the pool during times when it's open and when it's closed. Carrying an adequate level of homeowner liability insurance—and following the rules to maintain coverage—is a measure of safety as well.

Pools are inherently unsafe, as evidenced by the thousands of unintentional injuries and deaths that the CPSC attributes to the use of private residential swimming pool use every year. But if you approach your ownership responsibility with that understanding and then apply that respect with a variety of measures that lessen the risks and hazards, you'll greatly reduce the chances of experiencing an accident. Building codes regulating pool construction and installation often dictate these safety-related features, helping explain why the number of private pool injuries and deaths have gone down, even as nearly 800,000 pools are added each year to the several million already in place.

**A solid fence on all sides** provides privacy for swimming and sunbathing, and it also keeps neighborhood children from venturing into danger. Most local codes require fences or walls around pools.

# Common Safety Practices

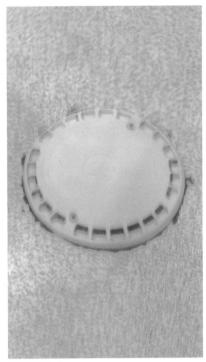

**A nonskid pool deck** is a requirement for a safe swimming area. Broomed concrete is a very popular choice because it is inexpensive and offers great traction even when it's wet.

**A sturdy ladder** with slip-resistant rungs or steps needs to be well-anchored to provide safe access.

**A dome-shaped drain cover** keeps objects and limbs from getting drawn into or snagged on the drain.

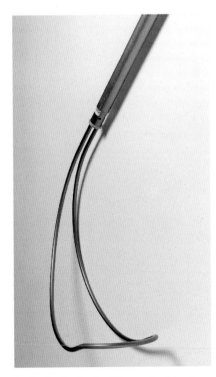

**A shepherd's hook** with a pole at least 12' long is vital as a tool for reaching a distressed swimmer.

**A wood fence near the pool area** is a handy spot to mount a waterproof first-aid kit.

**A self-closing gate latch** automatically catches and secures the latch when the gate swings shut.

# Treehouses

This section is all about the kids. One of the best ways to get children out from behind electronic screens and out of the house is to give them an outdoor structure where their imaginations can run wild. The structure doesn't necessarily have to be a palace in the sky or the Taj Mahal; it just needs to accommodate whimsical play, be durable, and—above all else—be entirely safe to use.

To make sure you hit the mark in creating the ideal treehouse, include your little ones (or not-so-little ones) in the design and even some aspects of the building process. Keep in mind that the final product doesn't necessarily need to look polished, as long as it suits the occupants for which it's intended.

That said, the trick is to design and build a treehouse that is large enough to foster imaginative play for multiple children, while still being small enough not to overshadow other features in your landscape. It also should not be so complex that you become overwhelmed midway through the construction. Basic straight lines, cut-out windows, and fundamental butt joints are going to be the order of the day; the point is to get the structure built rather than take a great deal of time fussing over details that might not matter at all to the youngsters using the structure.

No matter what, though, never sacrifice safety to expediency, especially with a treehouse. It's crucial that everything you do and build be in line with best standards and practices. The play structure should be securely attached to a tree or foundation, and should have no sharp exposed fasteners or rough wood edges that could lead to splinters.

# Treehouses

A treehouse is the ultimate un-house. For kids, it's a room that never has to be cleaned. A place for muddy shoes and bug jars and a pocketknife stuck into the wall. A house that you can paint whenever and however you want, without gaining approval. For adults, it's a room that never has to be cleaned, a place for muddy shoes and...well, you get the idea. But best of all a treehouse is up in a tree. And that's just cool.

This section walks you through the whole process. First, you'll select a tree (or trees). Don't worry if your yard isn't blessed with the perfect specimen; there are ways around the arboreally challenged. Then you'll design the structure to fit the site and, finally, build it to last.

Finding your host tree is a critical first step in the treehouse planning process. If your host tree isn't up to the task, you'll have to consider a smaller treehouse, or design in some auxiliary posts for structural support.

For most treehouse builders, the tree selection process (and the design selection process that follows) is less of a question of which tree to use than it is an assessment of whether a particular tree is a suitable candidate. While the viability of your structure is the key point, don't neglect to include the health of the tree when making your assessment. You don't want to kill your one beloved tree by burdening it with a structure that is, relative to the lifespan of the tree, temporary.

Many treehouses have been built successfully by incorporating more than one tree into the design. This is usually a good idea from a strength standpoint. However, designing the treehouse can be a lot like working by committee, since trees, like people, tend to act independently when the going gets tough.

Following are some general tips and rules to help you find a suitable host for the treehouse of your dreams. But before you start, there's this advice (it won't be the last time you hear it): When in doubt, ask an arborist. They're in the phone book, they're not expensive, and they can advise you on everything from tree diagnosis to healthy pruning to long-term maintenance.

## HOW BIG SHOULD A TREE BE?

Here are some general guidelines for assessing whether a tree meets minimum size requirements for your treehouse. It is assumed that the tree being considered is mature and healthy and that the treehouse you're planning is a moderately sized (100 sq. ft. or so), single-story structure.

- A single tree that will be the sole support for the house should measure at least 5 feet in circumference at its base.

- Main supporting limbs (where each limb supports one corner of the house's platform) should be at least 6 inches in diameter (19" circumference).

- Different types and shapes of trees have different strength characteristics—a professional's assessment of your tree can help you plan accordingly.

**Measure the circumference of any potential host tree** to determine if the tree is big enough to support your treehouse. For a normal-size treehouse, a single tree should be at least 5' in circumference at the base.

# General Tree Health

A tree doesn't have to be in the absolute prime of its life to be a suitable host for a treehouse, but it must be healthy. Other factors, such as location, can disqualify a candidate as decisively as its general health.

**Age.** Mature trees are best. They're bigger, stronger, and generally they move less in the wind than younger ones. They also have more heartwood (the hard, inner core of dead wood). When you drive a lag screw into a tree, it's the heartwood that really offers gripping power.

**Roots.** If your tree's root flares are buried from re-grading or gardening, take it as a warning sign that there might be problems below. Another thing to check for is girdling, where newer roots—often from nearby plants—have grown around the tree's primary anchoring roots, cutting off their life supply. Another warning sign: trees next to unpaved driveways or heavily trodden paths may have suffered damage from all the traffic.

**Trunk, branches, and leaves (or needles).** Inspect the largest members of the tree—the trunk and main branches. Look for large holes and hollow spots, rot on the bark or exposed areas, and signs of bug infestation. Check old wounds and damaged areas to see how the tree is healing. Avoid trees with a significant lean, as they are more likely to topple in a storm. When it comes to branches, look for stout limbs that meet the trunk at a near-perpendicular angle. Typically, the more acute the angle, the weaker the connection, although several suitable tree species naturally have branches set at 45 degrees. Dead branches here and there typically aren't a problem. These should be cut off before you start building. Finally, look at the canopy. In spring and summer the leaves should be green and full with no significant bare spots. Needles on evergreen trees should look normal and healthy.

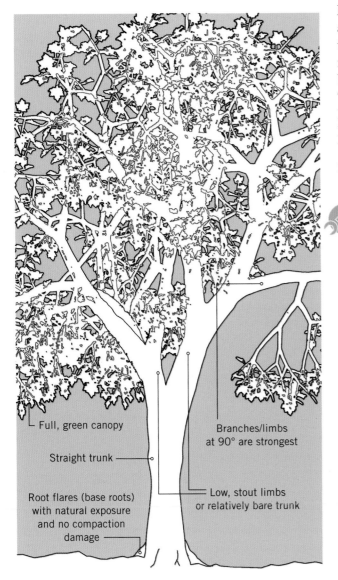

Full, green canopy

Straight trunk

Root flares (base roots) with natural exposure and no compaction damage

Branches/limbs at 90° are strongest

Low, stout limbs or relatively bare trunk

## TREE TIPS

- When you're building the treehouse and drilling holes for anchor screws, pay attention to the wood chips pulled out by the bit: granulated, dusty material indicates rot inside the tree and should be investigated further. Look for clean spirals and tough flakes or chips.

- Trees with multiple trunks often are fine for building in; however, the trunk junction is vulnerable to being pulled apart, especially under the added stress of a treehouse. The recommended remedy for this is to bind the tree up above with cables to prevent the trunks from spreading. This is a job for an arborist.

- To make sure your tree's foundation stays healthy, don't grow grass or add soil over the root flares. Keep shrubs and other competing plants outside of the ground area defined by the reach of the branches. And by all means, keep cars and crowds off the base roots, especially on trees with shallow root systems.

# Planning

If you built a treehouse as a kid you probably didn't spend a lot of time planning it beforehand. You had plenty of ideas and knew what you wanted—a trap door, a lookout post, a tire swing, and maybe a parachuting platform or helicopter pad—you just weren't exactly sure how everything would come together. In the end, you decided to figure it out along the way and got started.

Of course, some people might use the same approach today (good luck on the helicopter pad), but be advised that a little planning up front could save your project from disaster. Remember the guy with the metal clipboard from the city office? You don't want him showing up with a demolition order just as you're nailing up the last piece of trim.

Take time at the beginning of your project to address some basics, including general design features such as the size and style of the treehouse, where it

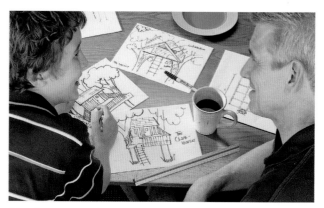

**Planning your treehouse** can be as much fun as building it, or even using it, if you choose to involve everyone and make it into a teaching/learning experience. After all, you're never too young to learn about building codes and zoning laws.

will sit in the tree, and how you'll get from the ground to the front door—if you want a front door.

NOTE: Before refining your treehouse plans, read the remainder of this section for important safety-related design considerations.

# Building Codes & Zoning Laws

When it comes to building codes and treehouses, the official word is that there is no official word. Many municipalities—the governing powers over building and zoning laws—consider treehouses to be "temporary" structures when they fit within certain size limits, typically about 100 to 120 square feet and not more than 10 to 12 feet tall. If you have concerns about the restrictiveness of the local laws, keeping your treehouse within their size limits for temporary structures is a good precaution to take.

When it comes to zoning laws, the city planning office is concerned less with a treehouse's construction and more with its impact on your property. They may state that you can't build anything within 3 feet or more of your property line (called setback restriction) or that you can't build a treehouse in your front yard (the Joneses might not be the treehouse type).

The bottom line is this: your local planning office might require you to get a building permit and pass inspections for your treehouse, or they might not care what you do, provided you keep the building within specific parameters. It's up to you to learn the rules. Although city laws are all over the map regarding treehouses, here are a few common-sense tips that are worth following no matter where you live.

- Talk with your neighbors about your treehouse plans. A show of respect and diplomacy on your part is likely to prevent them from filing a complaint with the authorities.

- Use discretion when selecting locations for windows (and decks) in your treehouse. Your neighbors might be a touch uncomfortable if you suddenly have a commanding view of their hot tub or a straight shot into their second-story windows.

- Electrical and plumbing service running to a treehouse tells the authorities that you plan to live there, thus your house crosses a big line from "temporary structure" to "residence" or "dwelling" and becomes subject to all the requirements of the standard building code.

- Don't build in a frontyard tree or other locations that are easily viewed from a public road. The point is not to hide from the authorities, it's that conspicuous treehouses attract too much attention and curiosity for the city's comfort, and the house might annoy your neighbors.

- In addition to keeping the size of your treehouse reasonable, pay attention to any height restriction for backyard structures. Treehouses can easily exceed these, for obvious reasons, but nevertheless may be held to the same height limits as sheds, garages, and other types of buildings.

- Even if the local building laws don't cover treehouses, you can look to the regular building code for guidance. It outlines construction standards for things like railings, floor joist spans, and accommodations for local weather and geologic (earthquake) conditions.

# Treehouse Safety

The fact is, a house up in a tree comes with some risks. But so does an elevated deck off of your kitchen or a jungle gym in your backyard. What makes you comfortable using any part of your house on a daily basis is your knowledge that it was designed thoughtfully to prevent common hazards. Performing conscientious, regular maintenance of a treehouse, or any other structure, ensures its safety and helps protect your peace of mind. The same applies to treehouses, although treehouses present an additional safety consideration—building off the ground.

Treehouse safety can be divided into two categories: safe design and safe working conditions. Both are equally important and perfectly manageable, and both should be followed regardless of who uses the house. A kids' treehouse naturally involves more safety concerns than one used exclusively by adults. However, keep in mind that you never know when children might visit, and it's too late once they're up

**A safe design and safe building practices** are essential to a successful treehouse project. Building a backyard structure is a great chance to involve kids and show them the right way to work with tools.

there. It's like bringing a two-year-old into a non-baby-proofed home. The adults are suddenly scrambling madly as they discover all the things that are perfectly safe for them but potentially deadly for a toddler.

# Safe Treehouse Design

The primary safeguard on any treehouse is the supporting platform. It alone keeps the house and its occupants aloft. Even if every other element is designed to the highest standards, a treehouse is completely unsafe if the platform isn't sound. Later information covers platform construction in detail, so for now, just two quick reminders:

1. Build platforms for kids' treehouses no higher than 8 feet above the ground.

2. Inspect the platform support members and tree connections regularly to make sure everything's in good shape.

With a strong, stable platform in place, you can turn your attention to the other elements of safety in design.

**Everything's riding on the treehouse platform.** Be sure to design and build it sturdily.

**A sturdy handle** is a welcome sight to tired climbers. Make sure all handles and mounting hardware are galvanized or otherwise corrosion-protected.

## Access Landings

Each type of access to a treehouse—ladder, rope, stairs, etc.—has its own design standards for safety, but all must have a landing point for arriving and departing. In many cases, the landing necessitates a gap in a railing or other opening and thus a potential fall hazard. Keep this in mind when planning access to your treehouse, and consider these recommendations:

- Include a safety rail across openings in railings (this is a must, not an option).

- Leave plenty of room around access openings, enough for anyone to safely climb onto the treehouse platform and stand up without backing up.

- Consider non-slip decking on landings to prevent falls if the surface gets wet.

- Add handles at the sides of access openings and anywhere else to facilitate climbing up and down; handholds cut into the treehouse floor work well, too.

- Install a safety gate to bar young children from areas where there are access openings.

## Windows & Doors

The obvious safety hazard for windows and doors is glass. So the rule is: don't use it, especially in kids' treehouses. Standard glass is too easily broken during play or by swaying branches or rocks thrown by taunted older brothers. Instead, use strong plastic sheeting. The strongest stuff is ¼-inch-thick polycarbonate glazing. It's rated for outdoor public buildings, like kiosks and bus stops, so it can easily survive the abuse from your own little vandals. Plastic does get scratched and some becomes cloudy over time, but it's easily replaceable and is better than a trip to the emergency room.

Even more important than the glazing is the placement of doors and windows. All doors and operable windows must open over a deck, not a drop to the ground. If a door is close to an access point, make sure there's ample floor space between the door and any opening in a railing, for example.

## Ground Below the Tree

Since occasional short falls are likely to occur when kids are climbing around trees, it's a good idea to fill the area beneath your treehouse with a soft ground cover. The best material for the health of the tree is wood chips. A 6-inch-thick bed of wood chips effectively cushions a fall from 7 feet, according to the National Resource Center for Health and Safety in Child Care. Also, keep the general area beneath the house free of rocks, branches, and anything else one would prefer not to land on.

**A soft bed of loose ground cover** is recommended under any kids' treehouse or areas where kids will be climbing.

Locking up may seem unnecessary for most backyard hideaways, but for some treehouses it's a sensible precaution. For example, treehouses located out of your daily view, especially those near a public road, can attract a lot of negative attention, like vandalism. More importantly, kids just can't resist getting into stuff, and you don't want to face a lawsuit because you made it easy for them to waltz into your house and get hurt. Of course, you had nothing to do with it. But try telling that to a plaintiff lawyer.

These are just suggestions, not legal advice:

- Install a strong door with a padlock (¾" plywood backed by a lumber frame is a good choice; it may be ugly, but it's strong).

- Post signage stating "No Trespassing," "Private Property," "Danger," or similar warnings.

- Install window shutters that lock on the inside or can be padlocked from the outside.

- Use plastic instead of glass in windows (the polycarbonate glazing mentioned on page 126 won't be broken with rocks).

- Use a retractable or removable ladder as the only means of access, and take it away when you leave the treehouse.

## Construction Details

One of the first rules of building children's play structures is to countersink all exposed fasteners. For good reason. If you fall and slide along a post, you might get a scrape and some splinters, but you're much better off than if your kneecap hits a protruding bolt on the way down. Follow the countersink rule for all kids' treehouses.

Speaking of splinters, take the time to sand rough edges as you build your house. Your kids and guests will be glad you did. Also keep an eye out for sharp points, protruding nails, and any rusty metal.

## Maintenance

Treehouses fight a constant battle with gravity. This, combined with outdoor exposure and the threat of rust and rot make regular inspections of the house a critical safety precaution. Inspect your treehouse several times throughout the year for signs of rot or damage to structural members and all supporting hardware. Also check everything after big storms and high winds, as excessive tree movement can easily cause damage to wood structures or break anchors without you knowing

it. Test safety railings, handholds, and access equipment more frequently.

Inspect the tree around connecting points for stress fractures and damage to the bark. Weighted members and tensioned cables and ropes rubbing against the bark can be deadly for a tree if it cuts into the layers just below the bark. Check openings where the trunk and branches pass through the treehouse, and expand them as needed to avoid strangling the tree. Finally, remove dead or damaged branches that could fall on the house.

**Neglected support beams and connections** are the most common causes of treehouse disasters. Check these parts often for rot, corrosion, and damage and replace immediately if evidence is found.

# Working Safely

Off-the-ground work has its own long list of safety guidelines on top of the regular set of basic construction safety rules. Since you can learn about general tool and job site safety anywhere (please do so), the focus here is on matters specific to treehouse building and related gravity-defying feats. But here are some good points to keep in mind.

Working outdoors presents challenges not faced in the interior, such as dealing with the weather, working at heights, and staying clear of power lines. By taking a few common-sense safety precautions, you can perform exterior work safely.

Dress appropriately for the job and weather. Avoid working in extreme temperatures, hot or cold, and never work outdoors during a storm or high winds.

Work with a helper whenever possible—especially when working at heights. If you must work alone, tell a family member or friend so the person can check in with you periodically. If you own a cell phone, keep it with you at all times.

Don't use tools or work at heights after consuming alcohol. If you're taking medicine, read the label and follow the recommendations regarding the use of tools and equipment.

When using ladders, extend the top of the ladder 3 feet above the roof edge for greater stability. Climb on and off the ladder at a point as close to the ground as possible. Use caution and keep your center of gravity low when moving from a ladder onto a roof. Keep your hips between the side rails when reaching over the side of a ladder, and be careful not to extend yourself too far or it could throw off your balance. Move the ladder as often as necessary to avoid overreaching. Finally, don't exceed the work-load rating for your ladder. Read and follow the load limits and safety instructions listed on the label.

**During construction,** ladder management is an exceptionally important aspect of jobsite safety. Since trees generally do not afford flat, smooth areas for the ladder rungs to rest, adding padded tips will help stabilize the ladder. And remember: a fall of just a couple of feet from a ladder can cause a fractured elbow or worse.

## Hardhat Area (Heads Up!)

The general area underneath the tree should be off limits to anyone not actively working on the project at hand. Someone walking idly underneath to check things out might not be engaged enough to react if something falls. Hardhats are a good idea for anyone working on the project and for kids anywhere close to the job site.

To keep an extension cord from dropping—and sometimes taking your tool with it—wrap the cord around a branch to carry the bulk of the weight. Also, wear a tool belt to keep tools and fasteners within reach while keeping your hands free to grab lumber, etc.

## Pulley Systems

A pulley is one of the fun features found on a lot of treehouses. They're great for delivering baskets full of food and supplies. During the build, a simple pulley set up with a bucket or crate is handy for hauling up tools and hardware.

Here's an easy way to set up a simple, lightweight pulley:

1. Using a strong nylon or hemp rope (don't use polypropylene, which doesn't stand up under sun exposure), tie one end to a small sandbag and throw it over a strong branch.

2. Tie a corrosion-resistant pulley near the end of the rope, then tie a loop closer to the end, using bowline knots for both.

3. Feed a second rope through the pulley and temporarily secure both ends so the rope won't slip through the pulley.

4. Thread the first rope through the loop made in step 2, then haul the pulley up snug to the branch. Tie off the end you're holding to secure the pulley to the branch.

For heavy-duty lifting, use a block and tackle, which is a pulley system that has one rope strung through two sets of pulleys (blocks). The magic of multiple-pulley systems is that the lifting power is increased by 1× for each pulley. For example, a block and tackle with six pulleys gives you 6 pounds of lifting force for each pound of force you put onto the pulling rope. If you weigh 150 pounds and hang on the pulling end, you could raise a nearly 900-pound load without moving a muscle. The drawback is that you have to pull the rope six times farther than if you were using a single pulley. For a high treehouse, you'll need a lot of rope.

When hauling up loads with a block and tackle, try to have a second person on the ground to man a control line tied to the load. This helps stabilize the load and steer it through branches and other obstacles. Additional control like this makes it safer for those up in the tree.

**A block and tackle** makes it easy to lift heavy support beams and pre-built walls.

## ⚠ SAFETY CHECKLISTS

### Safe Design Checklist
- Platform no more than 8 ft. above ground (for kids' treehouse).
- Strong railings 36" high, with balusters no more than 4" apart.
- Continuous railing along all open decks and at sides of stairs.
- Safety rail across all access openings.
- No horizontal railing balusters.
- Large access landings with handles or handholds as needed.
- No ladder rungs nailed to tree.
- Non-slip decking around access openings.
- No glass windows in kids' treehouses.
- Doors and operable windows open onto a deck, not a drop.
- Soft ground cover beneath kids' treehouses.
- Fasteners countersunk in all exposed areas.
- No rough wood edges, sharp points, or protruding nails or screws.
- Screws and bolts only for structural connections to tree; no nails.
- Regular maintenance check of platform support members and tree connections, railings, access equipment, and handles.
- Refer to local building codes for your area.

### Safe Construction Checklist
- Safety ropes and harness for any high work.
- Tie onto safety line even after platform is complete.
- No kids or visitors under tree during construction.
- Hardhats for workers on ground and all kids.
- Follow basic construction safety and ladder safety rules.

# Platform Basics

A typical treehouse platform is made up of support beams and a floor frame. The beams are anchored to the tree and carry the weight of the entire structure. The frame is made up of floor joists that run perpendicular to the beams. Topped with decking, the floor frame becomes the finished floor of the treehouse, onto which you build the walls and everything thereafter. Some small kids' treehouses have only a floor as the supporting structure, particularly when the house is low to the ground and is well-supported by branches.

Sizing beams and floor joists isn't an exact science, as it is with a regular house, but standard span tables can give you an idea about load limits for your treehouse. Contact your local building department for span tables and materials requirements for beams (also called girders), floor joists, and decking materials. What's unique to treehouses is the additional stress of the tree's motion and possible twisting forces applied to the floor frame. Flexible anchors are the best defense against tree motion, as you'll see later. In any case, it's better to err on the side of oversized support members.

The trick to building a successful platform is not just in the strength and stability. The platform must also be level. If you've ever been in an old house with a sloping floor, you know why. It messes with your sense of equilibrium and gives you an uneasy "funhouse" feeling. In a treehouse this can lead to a perceived sense of instability, plus it gives your friends and family something to make fun of. One handy technique for locating anchor points to create a level platform is to set up a mason's string and line level.

A few more tips for building platforms:

- Use a single ¾"-dia. galvanized lag screw to anchor lumber directly to the tree. For lightweight supports, you can get away with ½" lag screws, but don't use anything smaller.

- If a situation calls for more than one screw in any part of the tree, never place two screws in a vertical line less than 12" apart. To the tree, each screw is treated as a wound; if the screws are too close together, the wounds might coalesce, causing the area to rot.

- Never remove bark to create a flat surface for anchoring, etc. If done carefully, it's okay to shave the surface slightly, but always leave the protective layer of bark intact. A better solution is to use wood wedges to level out brackets and other anchors.

- When you're building a platform up in the tree, it's often helpful to cut beams or joists long at first, allowing some play as you piece the frame together. Cut off the excess after the framing is completed, or leave beam ends long to use as outriggers for pulleys, swings, etc.

**Fasteners placed close together** in a vertical line can lead to rot in the tree, causing the anchors to fail.

# Platform Anchoring Techniques

Anchoring the platform is all about dealing with tree movement. Here's the problem: if you're building in or around a section of the tree that's used to moving a lot in the wind and you tie multiple parts of the tree (or parts of different trees) together, something's got to give. Usually it's your platform's support beams or anchors that lose the battle by breaking or simply shearing off. The best solution is to respect Mother Nature by using anchors that make allowances for movement.

Treehouse builders have come up with a range of anchoring methods for different situations, but most fall into one of the four categories shown here. Knowing the main types of anchors will help you decide what's best for your project. Often a combination of different anchors is the most effective approach.

## Fixed Anchor

A fixed anchor is the most basic type, with the support beams firmly anchored to the tree with large lag screws. Because they allow for zero tree movement, fixed anchors are typically used on single-tree houses anchored exclusively to the trunk, or perhaps used in conjunction with a flexible anchor (sliding or hanging—see page 132) at the opposite end of the beam.

To install a fixed anchor, drill a slightly oversized hole for a lag screw through the beam, just below the center of the beam's depth. Drill a pilot hole into the tree that's slightly smaller than the screw's shank. Add one washer on the outside of the beam and one or two large, thick washers on the tree side, and anchor the beam to the tree with the lag screw. The washers on the tree side of the beam help prevent chafing of the beam against the bark.

Sizing the screw: Use a ¾-inch galvanized lag screw that's long enough to penetrate at least 5 to 6 inches into the tree's solid wood. Accounting for a 2× (1½-inch-thick) beam, the washers, and the bark, you need at least a 9-inch screw for a major beam connection.

Centerline of beam

Centerline of screw hole

**A single lag screw** is an adequate fixed anchor for a beam, provided the screw is heavy enough. Multiple screws can cause damage to your tree. Thread a washer between the screw head and the beam, and add at least a couple washers between the beam and the tree to prevent the beam from rubbing against and damaging the bark.

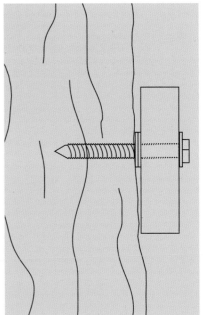

**A slot-type sliding anchor** allows single-directional movement between the tree or trees and the platform beams.

**A bracket-type sliding anchor** allows two-directional movement while offering solid support. Unfortunately, you'll have to have these custom-fabricated at a local metal shop.

3" to 6"

Screw eye

Shackle

Nut and bearing plate

**A screw eye or through bolt hanging anchor** requires a tree limb at least 6" in diameter.

**Knee braces support the platform,** distributing the load onto the trunk and off of the lag screws that attach the beams to the tree trunk.

# Platform Designs

**A single-tree platform** nestled in tree branches has a sturdy floor frame made from 2 × 6s and anchored directly to the tree.

**Single tree with trunk as center post** has a joist frame that rests on a pair of parallel supports that are bolted to the trunk. Braces running from the outer frame joists to the tree trunk stabilize the frame.

**A platform spanning two tree trunks** is supported by parallel 2 × 10 beams that are attached to both trunks. V-braces stabilize the outside joist frame members.

**Two trees and two support posts** give direct support to every corner of the treehouse platform. Posts should be set on a concrete pier that extends below the frostline.

# Installing Decking

If you're thinking that you've just jumped from platform beams to decking and skipped the floor framing, you're right. Because the configuration of the floor framing tends to follow the platform design, you'll get a better picture of that with the individual platform overviews on page 133.

Most treehouse platforms are decked using standard decking techniques. It's a lot like decking a . . . well, a deck, or a floor, depending on the materials used. Standard decking materials include 5/4 × 6 decking boards, 2 × 6 lumber, and ¾-inch exterior-grade plywood. Of these, plywood is the cheapest and easiest to install, but it comes with one drawback: treehouse floors tend to get wet, and the water has no place to go on a solid plywood surface. By contrast, decking boards can—and should—be gapped to allow water through and eliminate pooling. If you're really committed to creating a dry interior on

your house, you might consider plywood or tongue-and-groove decking boards, which make a smooth, strong floor without gaps.

Install decking boards with deck screws driven through pilot holes (although you would normally nail tongue-and-groove boards). Use screws that are long enough to penetrate the floor framing by at least 1¼ inch. Gap the boards ¼ inch apart, or more, if desired. Two screws at each joist are sufficient. Install plywood decking with 2-inch deck screws, driven every 6 inches along the perimeter and every 8 inches in the field of the sheet.

To allow for tree growth, try to leave a 2-inch gap between the decking and the tree. This means you'll have to scribe the decking and cut it to fit around tree penetrations. To scribe a board, set it on the floor as close as possible to its final position, then use a compass to trace the contours of the tree onto the board.

**Fasten the decking to the floor frame** with corrosion-resistant deck screws. Below: Use a compass to scribe decking boards at tree penetrations.

2" gap

# Framing Walls

In the interest of making friends with gravity, treehouse walls are typically framed with 2 × 2 or 2 × 3 lumber, as opposed to the standard 2 × 4 or 2 × 6 framing used in traditional houses. Single-story treehouses can usually get away with 24 inches on-center stud spacing instead of the standard 16-inch spacing. However, the siding you use may determine the spacing, as some siding requires support every 16 inches.

How tall you build the walls is up to you. Standard wall height is 8 feet. Treehouses have no standard, of course, but 6 to 7 feet gives most people enough headroom while maintaining a more intimate scale appropriate for a hideaway. Another consideration is wall shape. Often two of the four walls follow the shape of the roof, while the two adjacent walls are level across the top.

## Basic Wall Construction

A wall frame has horizontal top and bottom plates fastened over the ends of vertical studs. Where a window is present, a horizontal sill and header are installed between two studs to create a rough opening (door rough openings have only a header, along the top). On treehouses, similar framed openings can be used to frame around large tree penetrations.

In a four-walled structure, two of the walls are known as "through" walls and two are "butt" walls. The only difference is that through walls overlap the ends of the butt walls and are made longer to compensate for the thickness of the butt walls. For simplicity, the two through walls and two butt walls oppose each other so that both members of each type are made the same length.

**Build stud walls on the ground** and then lift them up onto the platform one wall at a time. Below: Through walls overlap butt walls and are fastened together to form a corner of the house.

Butt wall

Through wall

**Assemble the wall frame with screws or nails.** Add short cripple studs to continue the general stud layout at window and door openings.

To build a wall frame, cut the top and bottom plates to equal the total wall length (not counting the siding and trim). Lay the plates together on the ground—or driveway or garage floor—with their ends even. Mark the stud layout onto the plates, using 16- or 24-inch on-center spacing. Mark for an extra stud at each side of window and door openings; these are in addition to, and should not interrupt, the general stud layout. If you plan to install interior paneling or other finish, add an extra end stud to each end of the through walls. This gives you something to nail to when the walls are fitted together. Extra studs might also come in handy for nailing exterior siding.

Cut the studs to equal the total wall height minus 3 inches, the combined thickness of the plates. Position the plates over the ends of the studs, and fasten them with two 3-inch galvanized wood screws or deck screws driven through pilot holes. You can screw through the plates into the ends of the studs, or angle the screws (toenail) through opposing sides of the studs and into the plates. You can also use 10d or 16d galvanized nails instead of screws.

To frame a window opening, measure up from the bottom of the bottom plate, and mark the sill and header heights onto both side studs.

NOTE: If you're using a homemade window, make the rough opening 1½" wider and 2¼" taller than the finished (glazed) window dimensions.

This accounts for the window jambs made from ¾-inch-thick lumber and a sill made from 2 × 4 lumber. If you're using a recycled window sash (without its own frame), make the rough opening 1¾ inches wider and 2½ inches taller than the sash. Cut the sill and header and install them between the side studs, making sure the rough opening is perfectly square. Install short cripple studs below the sill and above the header to complete the general stud layout. Follow the same procedure to frame a rough opening for a door, making it 2½ inches wider and 1¼ inches taller than the finished door opening ( for a homemade door).

# Building Railings

A railing is primarily a safety device. All too often, amateur and even professional designers (especially professional designers) see railings as an opportunity to get creative. The result is an unsuitable railing, which is essentially useless. Build a strong, solid railing with closely spaced balusters and you won't have to worry about who uses the treehouse, whether it's small children or tipsy adults. That means no ropes, no cables, and no twigs. Okay. Lecture over.

A good treehouse railing employs the basic construction details of a standard deck railing. Many treehouse railings are even simpler, eliminating features like the broad horizontal cap rail commonly found on house decks. The important thing is to adhere to the following basic design requirements:

- Tops of railings must be at least 36" above the platform surface.

- Balusters (vertical spindles) may be spaced no more than 4" apart.

- Horizontal balusters are unsafe for children, who like to climb them.

- Railing posts (4 × 4 or larger lumber) may be spaced no more than 6' apart and must be anchored to the platform frame, not the decking.

- Top and bottom rails should be installed on the inside faces of railing posts.

- Balusters should be fastened with screws; if nails are used, balusters must be on the inside of horizontal rails.

- All openings in railings—for access to the treehouse platform—must have a safety rail across the top.

To build a simple railing, cut 4 × 4 support posts to extend from the bottom edge (or close to the edge) of the platform's floor joists to 36 inches above the decking surface. Anchor the posts on the outside of the joists with pairs of ½-inch carriage bolts with washers. Install posts at the ends of railing runs and every 6 feet in between, and at both sides of access openings and stairways.

Cut 2 × 4 or 2 × 6 horizontal rails to span between the top ends of the posts. Fasten the rails to the inside faces of the posts with pairs of 3-inch deck screws. Continue the rail through access openings to create a safety barrier. Mark the baluster layout onto the outside faces of the rails, spacing the balusters no more than 4 inches apart. Cut 2 × 2 balusters to extend from the top of the rail down to the floor framing, overlapping the joists by at least 4 inches. Fasten the balusters to the rails and joists with pairs of 2½-inch deck screws driven into pilot holes at each end.

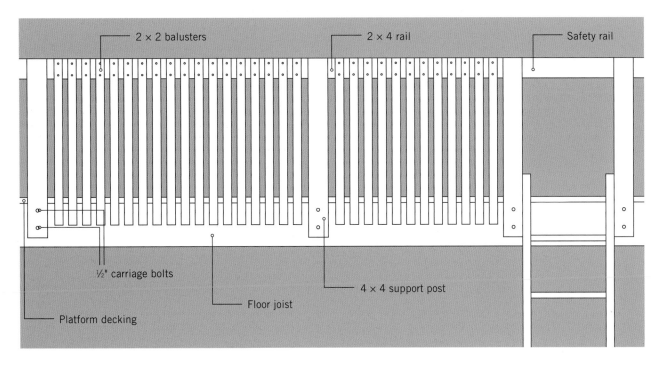

# Building Roofs

A treehouse roof is constructed just as any other small outbuilding roof, with the possible exception of the tree trunk that may project through it. If you are not experienced with building and covering roofs, consult an additional source for further information.

If you framed your walls with extreme care and everything came out square and perfectly level, you could design your roof frame on paper and use mathematical calculations to find all the angles and locate the necessary cuts. But because you're building in a tree, you're likely to have a better chance at success framing your roof using a cut-to-fit approach. The main structural members of any framed roof are the rafters and the roof deck, which is usually made from plywood roof sheathing.

On a gable roof, the rafters sit on top of the sidewalls and meet at a ridge board, or ridge beam, at the roof's peak. Rafters on hip roofs also form a peak, meeting at a ridge beam, or more commonly in treehouses, at the tree's trunk. A shed roof has no peak, and the rafters simply span from wall to wall. A roof's overall strength is determined primarily by the size of rafters and how closely they're spaced. Because treehouses tend to be small buildings, their roofs are typically built with 2 × 3 or 2 × 4 rafters spaced 16 or 24 inches on center. Check with the local building department for rafter span recommendations for your area.

Choose a roofing material for the roof deck, or sheathing. If you're building a small treehouse, take the easy route and use plywood. On any house with a gable or shed roof, consider adding 1x trim up against the underside of the roof sheathing along the end walls, to hide the faces of the outer rafters. For roof coverings, your principal choices are asphalt shingles, cedar shingles, or metal roof panels.

**A shed roof** is the easiest to build among permanent roofs. It can be covered with just about any material, including shingles, roll roofing and roof panels.

# Treehouse Roof Options

**Gable roofs** are considered the most classic roof style, with angled wall sections at either end.

**A removable roof** made from canvas or a plastic tarp may be all you need to shelter a tree fort or sun deck.

**Hip roofs** are sloped on all sides and are more difficult to frame than sheds and gables.

**A conical roof** is an impressive way to top a rounded wall. They're built with closely spaced rafters fanning out from the roof peak.

# Conversions Charts

## CONVERTING MEASUREMENTS

| TO CONVERT: | TO: | MULTIPLY BY: |
|---|---|---|
| Inches | Millimeters | 25.4 |
| Inches | Centimeters | 2.54 |
| Feet | Meters | 0.305 |
| Yards | Meters | 0.914 |
| Square inches | Square centimeters | 6.45 |
| Square feet | Square meters | 0.093 |
| Square yards | Square meters | 0.836 |
| Cubic inches | Cubic centimeters | 16.4 |
| Cubic feet | Cubic meters | 0.0283 |
| Cubic yards | Cubic meters | 0.765 |
| Pounds | Kilograms | 0.454 |

| TO CONVERT: | TO: | MULTIPLY BY: |
|---|---|---|
| Millimeters | Inches | 0.039 |
| Centimeters | Inches | 0.394 |
| Meters | Feet | 3.28 |
| Meters | Yards | 1.09 |
| Square centimeters | Square inches | 0.155 |
| Square meters | Square feet | 10.8 |
| Square meters | Square yards | 1.2 |
| Cubic centimeters | Cubic inches | 0.061 |
| Cubic meters | Cubic feet | 35.3 |
| Cubic meters | Cubic yards | 1.31 |
| Kilograms | Pounds | 2.2 |

## LUMBER DIMENSIONS

| NOMINAL - US | ACTUAL - US (IN INCHES) | METRIC |
|---|---|---|
| 1 × 2 | ¾ × 1½ | 19 × 38 mm |
| 1 × 3 | ¾ × 2½ | 19 × 64 mm |
| 1 × 4 | ¾ × 3½ | 19 × 89 mm |
| 1 × 5 | ¾ × 4½ | 19 × 114 mm |
| 1 × 6 | ¾ × 5½ | 19 × 140 mm |
| 1 × 7 | ¾ × 6¼ | 19 × 159 mm |
| 1 × 8 | ¾ × 7¼ | 19 × 184 mm |
| 1 × 10 | ¾ × 9¼ | 19 × 235 mm |
| 1 × 12 | ¾ × 11¼ | 19 × 286 mm |
| 2 × 2 | 1½ × 1½ | 38 × 38 mm |

| NOMINAL - US | ACTUAL - US (IN INCHES) | METRIC |
|---|---|---|
| 2 × 3 | 1½ × 2½ | 38 × 64 mm |
| 2 × 4 | 1½ × 3½ | 38 × 89 mm |
| 2 × 6 | 1½ × 5½ | 38 × 140 mm |
| 2 × 8 | 1½ × 7¼ | 38 × 184 mm |
| 2 × 10 | 1½ × 9¼ | 38 × 235 mm |
| 2 × 12 | 1½ × 11¼ | 38 × 286 mm |
| 4 × 4 | 3½ × 3½ | 89 × 89 mm |
| 4 × 6 | 3½ × 5½ | 89 × 140 mm |
| 6 × 6 | 5½ × 5½ | 140 × 140 mm |
| 8 × 8 | 7¼ × 7¼ | 184 × 184 mm |

## METRIC PLYWOOD

| STANDARD SHEATHING GRADE | SANDED GRADE |
|---|---|
| 7.5 mm (⁵⁄₁₆") | 6 mm (⁴⁄₁₇") |
| 9.5 mm (³⁄₈") | 8 mm (⁵⁄₁₆") |
| 12.5 mm (½") | 11 mm (⁷⁄₁₆") |
| 15.5 mm (⅝") | 14 mm (⁹⁄₁₆") |
| 18.5 mm (¾") | 17 mm (⅔") |
| 20.5 mm (¹³⁄₁₆") | 19 mm (¾") |
| 22.5 mm (⅞") | 21 mm (¹³⁄₁₆") |
| 25.5 mm (1") | 24 mm (¹⁵⁄₁₆") |

## COUNTERBORE, SHANK & PILOT HOLE DIAMETERS

| SCREW SIZE | COUNTERBORE DIAMETER FOR SCREW HEAD | CLEARANCE HOLE FOR SCREW SHANK | PILOT HOLE DIAMETER | |
|---|---|---|---|---|
| | | | HARD WOOD | SOFT WOOD |
| #1 | .146 (⁹⁄₆₄) | ⁵⁄₆₄ | ³⁄₆₄ | ¹⁄₃₂ |
| #2 | ¼ | ³⁄₃₂ | ³⁄₆₄ | ¹⁄₃₂ |
| #3 | ¼ | ⁷⁄₆₄ | ¹⁄₁₆ | ³⁄₆₄ |
| #4 | ¼ | ⅛ | ¹⁄₁₆ | ³⁄₆₄ |
| #5 | ¼ | ⅛ | ⁵⁄₆₄ | ¹⁄₁₆ |
| #6 | ⁵⁄₁₆ | ⁹⁄₆₄ | ³⁄₃₂ | ⁵⁄₆₄ |
| #7 | ⁵⁄₁₆ | ⁵⁄₃₂ | ³⁄₃₂ | ⁵⁄₆₄ |
| #8 | ⅜ | ¹¹⁄₆₄ | ⅛ | ³⁄₃₂ |
| #9 | ⅜ | ¹¹⁄₆₄ | ⅛ | ³⁄₃₂ |
| #10 | ⅜ | ³⁄₁₆ | ⅛ | ⁷⁄₆₄ |
| #11 | ½ | ³⁄₁₆ | ⁵⁄₃₂ | ⁹⁄₆₄ |
| #12 | ½ | ⁷⁄₃₂ | ⁹⁄₆₄ | ⅛ |

# Resources

**BLACK+DECKER**
Portable power tools and more
www.blackanddecker.com

## PLAYGROUND SAFETY

**National Program for Playground Safety**
Thorough website covering all aspects of
playground safety standards, products,
and best practices
www.playgroundsafety.org

**Consumer Product Safety Commission**
www.cpsc.gov
*Outdoor Home Playground Safety
Handbook* by the Consumer Product
Safety Commission is availa ble at:
www.cpsc.gov/s3fs-public/324.pdf

**Safe Kids**
Nonprofit dedicated to keeping children
safe on the playground and beyond
www.safekids.org

**Playgrounds & Playground Equipment**
Full playground kits and individual
components
www.playstarinc.com

**SwingWorks**
Swing components, slides, accessories,
and hardware
www.swingworks.com

**Detailed Play Systems**
Full range of backyard play structure kits
and components
www.detailedplay.com

**Swingsetmall.com**
Wide selection of swings, zip lines, tube
slides, accessories, and more
www.swingsetmall.com

**Swing Kingdom**
Full range of play structures and
accessories
www.swingkingdom.com

**CedarWorks**
Indoor and outdoor all-wood playsets, play
structures, and playhouses
www.cedarworks.com

**RubberScapes**
Rubber mulch for playgrounds
www.rubberscapes.net

**Surface America**
Specialized surfacing for playgrounds and
other recreational surfaces
www.surfaceamerica.com

**GameTime**
Full range of synthetic playground
surfacing materials
www.gametime.com

## TREEHOUSE SUPPLIES

**Treehouse Supplies**
Hardware kits and individual hardware
components
www.treehousesupplies.com

## SKATEBOARD RAMPS

**Skate Ramp Parts**
Surfacing, plans, and accessories for
building your own skate ramps
www.skateramps.us

**Skatelite**
Surfacing product for skateboard ramps
www.skatelite.com

## BASKETBALL

**Versacourt**
Complete court surfaces for basketball
and other home sport courts
www.versacourt.com

**Goalrilla**
Basketball goals and hoops
www.goalrilla.com

**Snapsports**
Athletic surfaces for the home
www.snapsports.com

## BOCCE

**Boccemon.com**
Surfacing materials, supplies, and bocce
court plans
www.boccemon.com

**Da Vinci Bocce**
Bocce ball supplies
www.davincibocce.com

**United States Bocce Federation**
Rules, tournament listings, and other
information covering the sport of bocce
www.usbf.us

## GOLF

**TJB**
Putting green kits and supplies
shop.tjb-inc.com

**Pro Putt Systems**
Backyard and indoor putting greens,
strike mats, and accessories
www.proputtsystems.com

**Backyard Golf**
Putting green kits and supplies
www.backyardgolf.us

## HORSESHOES

**National Horseshoe Pitchers Association**
Rules, information, and other resources
www.horseshoepitching.com

## PICKLEBALL

**United States Pickleball Association**
Rules, store, and other relevant
information
www.usapa.org

**Pickle-Ball, Inc.**
Paddles, balls, nets, and information
about the game
www.pickleball.com

**Pickleball Central**
Full range of paddles, nets, balls, and
accessories
www.pickleballcentral.com

## SWIMMING POOLS

**Doughboy**
Manufacturer of aboveground pools;
contact for dealer near network
www.doughboypools.com

**Crestwood**
Manufacturer of wood-clad and traditional
aboveground swimming pools
www.crestwoodpools.com

**Leisure Pools**
Supplies fiberglass pools and water
features
www.leisurepoolsusa.com

**Endless Pools**
Smaller-than-average lap pools with
artificial currents
www.endlesspools.com

# Index

# Photography Credits

The Association of Pool and Spa
  Professionals
www.theapsp.org
703-838-0083
p. 110

Barbara Butler
www.barbarabutler.com
p. 23

Bob Scott/Getty Images
p. 77

Dennis MacDonald/Alamy Stock Photo
p. 95 (top)

Intex Pools
www.intexpools.com
p. 117

iStock Photo
p. 57, 72 (top right), 86 (top), 87 (top right
  and left), 88, 92, 93 (inset), 94 (bottom
  left), 97 (top), 106 (left)

My Life Photos/Alamy Stock Photo
p. 78-79

© Peter Mason
p. 120-121

Shutterstock
p. 6, 8, 20, 24, 50, 60, 63 (bottom
  right),109, 116, 118